Autobiography.

" Man's life's a book of history;

The leaves thereof are days;

The letters, mercies closely joined;

The title is, Thy Praise!"

AUTOBIOGRAPHY

OF

A SCOTCH LAD:

BEING

Reminiscences

OF

THREESCORE YEARS AND TEN.

"Hitherto hath the Lord helped."

GLASGOW:

DAVID BRYCE & SON.

1887.

CONTENTS.

A Prayer.

———◆———

" Cast out, dear Lord, from my poor heart,
   All things wherein Thou hast no part;
   And fill it, Lord, abundantly
   With all that keeps it near to Thee!
   Yea, rid me of myself and sin,
   That Thou alone may'st reign within!"

PREFACE.

AUTOBIOGRAPHER had no thought of publication. When the idea of writing down the principal events of his life took hold of his mind he considered it would be a profitable mental and moral exercise, fill up spare minutes, and give cause to raise an Ebenezer for every mile-stone.

The leadings of Providence are wonderful. The windings, little incidents, unlooked-for occurrences, changes, new scenes, chief events of history, as reviewed, give astonishment. All along the road, while there is much to humble, there has been much to excite in the mind grateful feelings.

It is with "fear and trembling" that this book is given to the public; but it owes its place in type to the good opinion of others, who considered it well adapted for general interest and usefulness.

The writer withholds his name, desiring as much as possible to hide himself behind Divine grace and goodness.

May God give His blessing, and make the "Autobiography" a spiritual good! Then there will be an abundant reward to him who writes these lines.

AUTOBIOGRAPHY.

CHAPTER I.

Birth and Parentage.

" Mark well the tiny voice, the plump, spread arms,
  The artless smile, the little sprawling feet,
And the fond mother gazing on its charms,
  Breathing her heart in music low and sweet.
They make a picture."

M. B., *EXCELSIOR.*

IRTH-DAYS and birth-places are full of interest. *Then* and *there* begins mysterious life, that has an importance that cannot be conceived — the immortal within commencing a history of untold issues.

Not a few chronicle with gratitude their natal day, have happy thoughts about their birth-home, and think of father and mother with ivy-fondness. Their parents may be in the grave; but are seen and heard with mental eye and ear, and the loving hand feels as if resting on the shoulder. It is so with a " Scotch lad."

B

The quiet town of Galston, Ayrshire, pleasantly situated by the river Irvine, and near to Loudoun Castle, was my birth-place. The natal day was 15th May, 1816. My parents were "righteous before God," and sought to train their children for Heaven.

Father was related to John Howie of Lochgoin, author of the "Scots Worthies," and in a large measure inherited the spirit of the Covenanters. When a young man, engaged in farm work, rather than attend the parish church he walked some eight or ten miles on the Lord's-day to worship in what was then called the Secession Church. Mother's name was Sarah Cameron, of Highland descent, whose parents attained a great age—one dying at the age of 98, the other at 103. The latter had second sight, and was able to read the smallest print without her spectacles.

Father was a shopkeeper, and was respected as a man of business. Some thought him too kind and forbearing with customers who were careless about their payments. His moral standing with the members of the Secession Church was such that he was elected an elder. The Sabbath school and other religious agencies engaged his loving attention.

The Rev. James Blackwood was my father's minister. When but a child, his stately well-formed figure and open kind face, enkindled within me awe and respect. In his yearly ministerial visitations it was the joy of my heart to have his kind word and the loving pat of his hand. He had a powerful voice, and in the pulpit spoke with

vehemence and earnestness. His discourses, as a
rule, were full of heads and particulars; and my
wonder is that father remembered them so as to write
them on his return home, which was his frequent
practice. Two manuscript volumes are in my possession. The Rev. David T. Jamieson, of Kilmarnock, in an "Address to the Rev. Mr. Mathieson, on
his being ordained pastor in connection with the
Rev. James Blackwood," in 1843, may well say:—
"It will, I have no doubt, be your delight, as it will
be your interest and duty, to revere, to love, and
consult your colleague—amiable for his many
Christian graces, and venerable for his grey hairs,
which are his crown of glory, because found in the
way of righteousness. You will find him willing
to give you his experience—no trifling gift to a
young minister of the Gospel. You will have in
him a 'home for your affections and a school for
your intellect.'" Truthful words; which doubtless
were as hidden treasure in the heart. The memory
of Mr. Blackwood has a fragance that can never be
lost.

I was named after my venerated father. Would
that I had possessed in a larger measure his spirit!
I remember with interest the particularness with
which the Sabbath was kept. No menial work was
permitted; the children were not allowed to cross
the front-door threshold, unless when going to
church; only strictly religious books were allowed
to be read; and on the eve of the sacred day the
family were catechized on the sermons heard, on
the Shorter Catechism, and on Bible subjects.

He was fond of books; for his day possessed a good library, and was intelligent and well versed in religious truth. There were in the town about a dozen kindred spirits who met and had Christian converse that made the heart glow heavenward. Family worship was faithfully observed. There was first the singing of a psalm or paraphrase in rustic music, then reading a chapter, afterwards an earnest prayer. Over and around the family were sacred influences.

The memories of childhood cannot be forgotten; and I feel thankful to God for such parents. Alas! I have to mourn over unworthiness and mis-improvement.

CHAPTER II.

First Years.

" 'Tis come—the hour
Sacred to culture ; now unto his soul
Exultingly expanding, as a flower
Opening its petals, is a wise control
As pruning to the plant—as genial shower
Instruction's voice instilling truth with power."

M. B., *Excelsior.*

"Be very vigilant over thy child in the April of his understanding, lest the frosts of May nip his blossoms ; while he is a tender twig, straighten him ; while he is a new vessel, season him ; such as thou makest him, such commonly shalt thou find him."—QUARLES.

FIRST years have great importance. They are the foundations of character, and not unfrequently forbode the future. The unheeded little eddies go on widening, and lose themselves in the ocean of eternity. Impulses first felt keep throbbing ; words first uttered give echoes ; actions first done leave their prints. My first days are linked to the after ones, and, together, make the chain of life. Under God I owe much—it may be everything—to them.

At the usual age I was sent to school, and received a simple and meagre education. The ordinary school code may be reckoned on three fingers—reading, writing, and arithmetic. There was a little spelling, and sometimes questions to answer from the Shorter Catechism, occasionally repeating a paraphrase. My conduct in the school was of the ordinary kind—not always what it should be—and it was my misfortune sometimes to be punished. Out of school I indulged in the usual sports, which occasionally ended in a fight, but never a serious one. Boys can weep and laugh, fight and shake hands, within a few minutes. The surly boy was the speckled one of the school, the good-natured boy was its sunshine. My old teacher died, and was succeeded by one who introduced new methods which were not always popular. Comparisons are odious, and ought to be avoided, but we boys freely made them between the old and new masters.

The Communion season was a time of interest. Although under ten years of age, my mind was variously excited by what I saw and heard. I could not then fully grasp the grand truth of Christ's sacrificial offering, and the indebtedness of His children to remember it in the Memorial Supper. I was not without serious thoughts; but it was the *outward* that principally attracted me.

On the morning of this Communion day, father's house was open to receive Christian friends from the country. Within it were much commotion, glad welcomes, and a cheerful ministering to their wants.

The meeting-house—the solemn-faced communicants sitting at the two or three long tables in front of the pulpit, extending from aisle to aisle, and covered with white cloth—the minister on an elevation speaking earnest, loving words—excited my attention. The first address being given, the bread and wine were carried round by the elders. After the communicants had partaken, there followed a second address; part of a psalm being sung as they quietly left the tables, making room for others; when the same order of service was gone through, another minister officiating. When the tables were again filled, a third minister presided, fulfilling the same duties. It may be there was a fourth table; for frequently the holy Communion was attended by hundreds who came together for miles round. Robert Burns may call such a season "The Holy Fair"—we call it the Passover Feast. Each minister spoke, from different standpoints, on the grand truth of God's love in the Person and Work of Christ and our obligations to Him, and gave fulness and variety to their Gospel utterances. Their appearance—the robes, solemn looks, gestures, intonations, and words—impressed me.

When the Communion service was going on in the Church, sermons were being preached by the ministers, in rotation, from the Tent. Hundreds were assembled on the green sward, some seated on chairs kindly given for the occasion, others standing, and not a few reclining on the grass. There was great attention, as was proved by eager looks and wet cheeks. Some careless ones were present, but the many were devout worshippers. A concluding service was held on Monday, when a sermon was preached.

The picture of such a time painted on the retina of the memory gives interesting and profitable thoughts. We would gladly have a renewal of these holy Communion seasons.

It is sad to relate that, notwithstanding religious advantages, I—from six to eleven years old—gave my parents much anxious concern. An ungodly boy, the pest of the town, had fascinated and entangled me, and with him I was running down to ruin. I remember the time when, for some serious fault, he was punished by being drummed through the streets, and afterwards put in prison. Alas! that such a boy should have been my companion, or that by him I should have been led into evil. On one occasion I ran away, wandered to Kilmarnock—a distance of about six miles—and gave my parents much uneasiness; but to their joy the runaway was found.

I am now full of questionings respecting this wicked lad. What became of him? Was he spared to reach manhood, or was he cut off in youth? Did he continue in wickedness, adding sin to sin; or, through the rich mercy of God, was he saved? Shall we meet in heaven washed in the blood of the Lamb, and be companions in glory? Grace has its marvels; and he may be one of them.

CHAPTER III.

The Great Change.

"And thou, my soul, inspired with holy flame,
   View and review, with most regardful eye,
That holy Cross whence thy salvation came,
   On which thy Saviour and thy sin did die;
For in that sacred object is much pleasure,
And in that Saviour is my life and treasure."
                              SIR WALTER RALEIGH.

THERE was a book in my father's library that seemed to command special attention about the year 1826. He was often reading it. It was Boston's "Crook in the Lot;" and was peculiarly adapted to his circumstances at the time; for he was then passing through deep waters of temporal trouble. His business had failed through losses and other causes; and, having a family of seven children, with "the wolf at the door," he was much perplexed. Methinks I see him standing mute before God. "I was dumb, I opened not my mouth; because Thou didst it." There was no murmuring. My father believed that it was of the Lord; and, though Providence now seemed dark and mysterious, he was convinced his trials were for his good. If "Boston's" book had its bitters, it had also its cordials. In the "Crook in the Lot" was rich consolation—mention made of a tree that sweetened bitter waters; breaks in the dark cloud, through which were seen loving Divine eyes.

A voice was heard as in Abram's case—" Get thee out of thy country, into a land that I will shew thee." My father had kind friends in Glasgow with whom he had done business, who were ready to help him; and he removed to the great commercial city.

To the family and myself the removal was a bright providence. I was delivered from the snare of my boy-fowler who had me in his sin-coils. The other members of the family had openings in business that they could not have had in Galston. Thus we were led by a right though crooked way; and may well erect grateful Ebenezers. "Jehovah-jireh"—The Lord will provide!

At this time I was about eleven years old. This proved the turning point in my life. I well remember the night before our removal. The Spirit of God was at work in my soul. My past life, my wicked ways, the great pain and anxiety I had given my parents, what a sinner I was in God's sight, rose in remembrance. Humbled and penitent I resolved, by Divine help, never more to be a grief to father and mother; and if spared to get to Glasgow to be careful in choosing my companions. In short, it was my purpose to turn over a new leaf, and with a clear page to seek to live to God's glory.

On arriving at the great city the vow was carefully, though imperfectly, fulfilled. God gave grace and strength. I became serious, read only the Bible and religious books; and not satisfied with morning and evening prayers, would — when opportunity offered—turn aside into secluded places, and there on bended knee pour out my soul to God. The books I specially delighted in were alarming in their character; such as Baxter's "Call to the Unconverted," Alleine's "Alarm to Unconverted Sinners," Law's "Serious Call," etc.; these gave a melancholy and legal tinge to my religious views.

At the age of thirteen I became a member of a Bible-class taught by Mr. John Paul, then known in Glasgow as "the Apostle of the Goose Dubs"—the name given to a low, degraded locality in the city. The class was attended principally by poor boys and some roughs; but there were others, like myself, differently circumstanced, who were not ashamed to sit on the same form with them, so that we might share the peculiarly gifted teaching of such a man.

When about fifteen years old my views of Gospel truth became changed. Up to this time I had austere notions, considering painful experiences essential. I thought I must weep over sin and have a sadly crushed spirit. To evoke within me these feelings, I read the awful portions of the Bible, alarming books, and would set apart hours to think over my sins and their consequences. Notwithstanding all efforts I never could experience the anguish I thought necessary, and was full of restlessness. At this time I bought Pike's "Persuasives to Early Piety," and Abbot's "Young Christian." Reading these I discovered my error, and was led to see by God's Holy Spirit that religion was sunny; that mental anguish was the slave of unbelief; that I had only to trust in the finished work of Christ to find joy and peace and eternal life. Great was the change in my thoughts. The clouds on my religious atmosphere were removed; I had a clear sky, and saw "light in God's light."

Although impressed with every page of the "Persuasives to Early Piety," yet there was in it this anecdote that was of peculiar service and help, showing that conversion is not the work of days or weeks, but immediate; and also teaching that, as in the case of the Philippian jailer, we may believe, receive, and rejoice at one and the same moment:—

"It is related that a pious minister of the 17th century, having finished prayer, observed a young gentleman just shut into one of the pews who discovered much uneasiness and seemed to wish to get out again. The minister felt a peculiar desire to detain him, and turning towards one of the members of his church who sat in the gallery, he asked him aloud, 'Brother, do you repent of your coming to Christ?' 'No, sir,' he replied; 'I never was happy till then; I only repent that I did not come to Him sooner.' The minister turned towards the opposite gallery, and addressed himself to an aged member: 'Brother, do you repent that you came to Christ?' 'No, sir,' said he; 'I have known the Lord from my youth up.' He then looked down upon the young man, whose attention was fully engaged, and fixing his eyes upon him, said: 'Young man, *are you* willing to come to Christ?' This unexpected address from the pulpit, exciting the observation of all, so affected him that he sat down and hid his face. The person who sat next to him encouraged him to rise and answer the question. The minister repeated it: 'Young man, *are you* willing to come to Christ?' With a tremulous voice he replied, 'Yes, sir.' 'But *when*, sir?' added the minister in a solemn and loud tone. He mildly answered, 'Now, sir.' 'Then stay,' said he, 'and hear the word of God, which you will find in 2 Cor. vi. 2: '*Behold, now is the accepted time; behold, now is the day of salvation.*' By this sermon he was greatly affected; he went into the vestry after service dissolved in tears. That unwillingness to stay which he had discovered was occasioned by the injunction of his father, who threatened that, if ever he went to hear the fanatics, he would turn him out of doors. Having now heard, and being unable to conceal the feelings of his mind, he was afraid to meet his father. The minister sat down and wrote an affectionate letter to him, which had so good an effect that both father and mother came to hear for themselves. They were both brought to the knowledge of the truth; and father, mother, and son were together received with universal joy into the church."

The passage in Abbot's "Young Christian," specially blessed, and leading me to see that prolonged compunction was an evil, indicative of unbelief, was as follows :—

"I doubt not now but that many of my readers who have taken up this book with a desire to find *religious instruction* in it, have been for some time wishing to have me come to the subject of the confession of sin to God. You feel that the greatest of all your transgressions have been against Him, and you can have no true peace of mind again until He has forgiven you. I have no doubt that this is the state of mind of very many of those who will read this chapter. But confession of sin is the same in its nature and tendency when made to God as when made to your fellow-man. When you have finished this chapter, then, shut the book and go alone before your Maker, and acknowledge all your sins. Acknowledge them frankly and fully, and try to see and feel the worst, not by merely calling your offences by harsh names, but by calmly looking at the aggravating circumstances. While you do this, do not spend your strength in trying to *feel strong emotion.* You cannot feel emotion by merely trying to do so. There is no need of any terror—no need of agony of body or of mind—no need of gloom of countenance or anxiety of heart. Just go and sincerely acknowledge your sins to God, and ask Him to forgive you through Jesus Christ, and He will.

"But perhaps some one of you may say, 'I am surprised to hear you say that there is no need of strong agitation of mind before we can be forgiven for sin. I am sure that there often is very strong feeling of this kind. There is terror and agony of mind, and afterwards the individual becomes a sincere Christian.'

"It is true. There is sometimes strong and continued agitation, but it is only because those who suffer it are unwilling to *yield to God* and confess their sins to Him. As soon as this unwillingness is gone, and they come to their God and Saviour with all their hearts, the mental suffering vanishes. I said that if you were *willing now* to confess your sins to God, with sincere penitence, you may at once be happy. Of course, if you are unwilling—if you see that you are sinning against Him, and will not come and make peace—you then have indeed cause to tremble.

" There is a great mistake prevalent on this subject, especially among the young, though the subject is often clearly enough explained, both from the press and the pulpit. God's command is, *repent at once*, and believe on the Lord Jesus Christ, and you shall have peace. I have in this chapter used the word confess instead of repent, for sincere confession is only a manifestation of penitence. Now, I do not find that the Bible requires anything *previous* to repentance. It does not say that we must be miserable a week, or a day, or an hour. I never heard any minister urge upon his hearers the duty of suffering anguish of mind, and all the horrors of remorse, a single moment in order to prepare the soul for Christ. It is doubtless true that persons do often thus suffer, and are perhaps led by it in the end to fly to the refuge. *But they ought to have fled to the refuge, without this suffering, in the beginning.* The truth is that God commands men everywhere to repent : it is a notorious fact that they will not comply. When the duty of humbly confessing their sins to God is clearly brought before them, there is often so great a desire to continue in sin that a very painful struggle continues for some time. Now this struggle is all our own fault; it is something that we *add* altogether; God does not require it. He says, Come to Me *at once*. Ministers in the pulpit do not urge it: so far from desiring it are they, that they always urge their hearers to come at once to the Saviour and be happy; and when any of their hearers are suffering in consequence of their indecision, the pastor, so far from wishing them to continue in this state as a part of their duty, urges them with all his power to terminate it at once, by giving up their hearts to God and to happiness. And yet so reluctant are men to give up their hearts to God, and so exceedingly common is this guilty struggle, that by the young it is often considered *as a painful part of duty*. They think they cannot become Christians without it. Some try to awaken it and continue it, and are sad because they cannot succeed. Others are serving their Maker, endeavouring to grow in grace and to prepare for Heaven; but they feel but little confidence in His sympathy or affection for them, because, just before they concluded to yield to God, sin did not make such violent and desperate efforts in their hearts as in some others to retain its hold.

" No, my reader, there is no need of any struggle or of any suffering. If this chapter has led you to be willing to confess your sins, you may confess them now, and from this moment be calm and peaceful and happy.

" My reader will recollect, that I mentioned in the early part of this chapter, two points connected with confession, viz., *reparation* and *punishment*. In confessing sins to God, we have no reparation to Him to make, and no punishment to suffer. We have a Saviour, and we fly to Him. He makes reparation, and He has already suffered for us. We must come trusting in Him. I hope very many of my readers will see that both duty and happiness urge them to take the simple course I have endeavoured to describe and illustrate, and that they will now take it, and follow me through the remaining chapters of this book, with hearts bent on loving and serving God."

These words were openings in my dark experience cloud; they were "Peace, be still," heard amid waves of mental conflict. Jesus *Himself*, walking on the stormy sea, said, "*Be of good cheer;*" dismiss all your fears: "*It is I,*" your Almighty and Gracious Saviour: "*Be not afraid;*" rejoice and feel that all is well.

Ah! how *near* and *immediate* is eternal life— quick as the glance of the eye.

> " There is life for a look at the Crucified One,
>   There is life at this moment for thee ;
> Then look, sinner, look unto Him and be saved,
>   Unto Him who was nailed to the tree."

CHAPTER IV.

Apprenticeship.

" Come to me often, sportive memory ;
 Thy hands are full of flowers ; thy voice is sweet ;
 Thine innocent, uncareful look doth meet
The solitary cravings of mine eye ;
I cannot let thee flit unheeded by,
 For I have gentle words wherewith to greet
Thy welcome visits."

REV. HENRY ALFORD.

IT was well that my father put me, at thirteen years of age, as an apprentice to learn the art of printing. The good hand of God was in it. The term was seven years. My duties had wholly to do with " composing," *i.e.*, arranging the letters or types in a composing stick.

" Pick and click goes the type in the stick,
 As the printer stands at his case ;
His eye glances quick, and his fingers pick
 The type at a rapid pace."

A printing office where there is book-work is the best of schools. The compositor may be ignorant of the rules of grammar, yet he must have in some measure a practical knowledge of orthography, etymology, and syntax. He must have a knowledge of punctuation. Many authors write their manuscript without points, and the compositor has to fill them in. He has also to know—it may be in a small measure—something of the Hebrew and the Greek letters. Besides he has to decipher all kinds of writings, sometimes very difficult to make out, but patience and use render the task somewhat easy. I well recollect the nice, clear, plain " hand " of the late Rev. Dr. Ralph Wardlaw, which was a pleasure to " set up;" and the strange, difficult-to-read writing of the late Rev. Dr. Thomas Chalmers.

It was my privilege to see many of the ministers of the Reformed Presbyterian body, who frequently called at the office. I remember, among others, the small, bent form—doubtless from old age—of the good Rev. Mr. Mason, of Wishaw, who wrote on the prophecies and other subjects, and the noble presence of the Revs. Messrs Rogerson and Symington.

The first years of my apprenticeship were spent in the printing office at the foot of the Candleriggs; afterwards, with the same master, in his larger premises at 75 Argyle Street. Both places are fraught with interest, and have memories that cannot be forgotten.

I desire to linger on these days, and recall past fellowships and

" The touch of a vanished hand,
And the sound of a voice that is still."

There was my old master, who in some way was related to my father. He hailed from Ayrshire, and was a true Covenanter, an elder in the Cameronian

Church, and firm to his principles. In the first year of apprenticeship, when called the "printer's devil," if I failed in duty his stern, rebuking voice made me tremble. He was a good man, interested in my welfare, and his rebukes were necessary discipline.

There was my young master. His father dying, the business for a time was conducted by him. A collegian of the United Presbyterian Church, he had to combine study with business. He was comely in look and kind-hearted. I can never forget his attentions. Being one of a select Christian band, that had David Nasmith, Esq., as its centre, he invited me to one of their meetings, when met for religious and philanthropic purposes. There were present beside my master and Mr. Nasmith a few choice spirits—men who were "the salt of the earth;" and to-day their names and forms and memories are present, and dear to me. It was a time of sacred interest.

Mr. Nasmith established and edited a weekly penny serial called *The Christian Philanthropist's Companion*, the first number of which was issued in September 14th, 1833. This publication sought to promote personal holiness and conse-cration, and certain Christian agencies. Its first address "to the Reader" is as follows :—

"The present are times in which every means should be used to stimulate and direct the Christian Philanthropist in his efforts to save a dying world. Time is short, and millions are dropping into hell. That overturning has commenced, and is advancing

with amazing speed, which shall precede the coming
of Him whose right it is to reign. *Now* is the
time in which the Christian Philanthropist may be
privileged to give himself up a living sacrifice to
God; his time, his prayers, his efforts, his money,
his skill and his influence, are all required, and
may now be consecrated to great advantage. The
doors of usefulness are innumerable; the calls from
all parts of the world—to him that has an ear to hear
are—'Come over and help;' and a large blessing
is in reserve to be bestowed in answer to the work
and prayer of faith.

"As the Bible is the heavenly guide of the
Christian Philanthropist, the *Companion* will
always commence with a short portion of Scripture,
setting forth some precept or example worthy of
special attention, and close with the verses which
the many thousands in Europe and America are
treasuring in their memory from week to week.

"The religious interests of Glasgow, from its being
the largest city in Scotland, and admitted by all to
be a city of no small influence, will ever meet with
special attention.

"Under the head of *Editor's Correspondence*
may occasionally be found communications, not of
very recent date, but such as contain information
that may interest and edify the reader. And to
meet the wishes of some, the Editor will
occasionally communicate under the head *Note
Book* portions of the information he derived and
some of the incidents that occurred in his travels in
Europe and America.

"It will be the aim of the Editor to render this work useful, by making it practical; and in doing so, he is fully aware that it will be impossible to please *all* his readers. His determination, however, is, according to the grace bestowed upon him, faithfully to discharge his duties not as pleasing men, but God who searcheth the heart. He will always feel grateful to Christians, especially experienced Christians, to point out any way by which the design of the work may be more fully attained."

It may interest the readers to know what Glasgow—in its population and Christian agencies—was fifty-three years ago. This information is given in the first number of *The Christian Philanthropist's Companion*, and is as follows:—

"The City of Glasgow contains a population of about 203,000. It has upwards of 50 churches; 21 city and nine Parochial missionaries; about 300 Sabbath-school teachers attended by about 12,000 pupils. It has 600 tract distributors who issue about 30,000 tracts monthly. It has about 20 Temperance Associations. It has two Young Men's Societies, with from 400 to 500 members, who meet in about 35 associations for mutual improvement, and doing good to those around them. It has two Young Women's Societies, embracing about 120 members, who meet in 17 associations for mutual improvement, and doing good to their own sex. It has four Associations of Mothers connected with the Maternal Society, who meet weekly to commend their offspring to God in prayer, and to consult as to the best means of fitting their children for usefulness

on earth, and for mansions in heaven. It has a
Children's Mission, for training the young to habits
of usefulness, whose missionary is engaged in visiting and dispensing blessings to the poor. It has
a Christian Instruction Society, whose voluntary
agents visit in districts unoccupied by the agents of
the City Mission. It has a Philanthropic Society,
which by a variety of means has been seeking to
promote a revival of religion ; and it has upwards of
100 fellowship or prayer meetings in different parts
of the city."

In this "Gospel City" of so many Christian
agencies it was necessary that the religious philanthropists should be well furnished for their work ;
hence Mr. Nasmith printed for their use a most
important book, headed, "Hints, designed to Aid
Christians in their Efforts to Convert Men to God.
By Thomas H. Skinner, Pastor of the Fifth Presbyterian Church, Philadelphia, and Edward Beecher,
President of Illinois College. With a Narrative of
the State of Religion in several of the Churches in
Philadelphia. By Ezra Stiles, Esq., editor of 'Visits
of Mercy.'" Thus this good man was indeed full
of work for Jesus ; and his influence for good, in
Glasgow and elsewhere, was immense. Many of
the religious agencies now in existence owe their
origin to him.

The race of my young master was soon run. The
hectic fire that helped to make his face shine was
coursing in his veins and consuming his vitals.
After finishing his course of studies he became
the minister of the Secession Church, Catrine ; but

this office he only filled for two or three years—his spirit was called to the higher ministrations of Heaven. He had a younger brother for whom the business was designed; but he, too, died in early life. I am told that one member of the family survives, and that her name is Lizzie. Soon she, too, will reach the happy home; and with the loved ones that are gone before, unite in praising matchless, redeeming love—that God who has done all things well.

Of my fellow-apprentices during the seven years' service, some are but as shadows in the memory, not distinctly remembered. Not so with two brothers who were pressmen. They were good and true, and I think of them with affection. Both left their " craft " for higher work. One became a pastor, the other a useful town missionary. They have ceased from labour and entered on their reward amongst the many we hope to meet in Spirit Land.

One apprentice has greater outness than they all. We were compositors together, and had our follies and freaks and enjoyments. He has risen to greatness in his art, being one of the principals in a large printing and stationery establishment. Thank God! he has even higher honours than those of business, adorned by a character that gives divineness. He is a United Presbyterian elder, and has to do with some of the Christian philanthropies of the city. I have his photo in my album. He there appears venerable and pleasant. There is the white hoar head; the grave and kindly and intelligent

lines of the face; and could we look into the eye—
the picture is not full-faced—methinks we would
see keenness for business softened by grace. My
prayer is that, united by apprenticeship and loving
affection on earth, our union may have the immortal
" crown of righteousness that fadeth not away."

CHAPTER V.

Christian Privilege and Work.

" I would not check the nobly good,
  Who joy diffusing, widely roam ;
But I would whisper if I could,
  Look round, for there are wrongs at home ;
And voices, though but feeble, call
On Heav'n, on thee, on me, on all."

BOWRING.

PROVIDENCE was kind! Coming from a small town in early life, with no experience, a member of an obscure family, a stranger, settling in the populous city of Glasgow, yet so soon introduced to Christian friends and religious society! It is a wonder that such should have been the case. Everywhere there were snares and temptations; the godless of both sexes were ready to lead astray; yet such were the gracious influences that surrounded me, that I never once fell into evil. It seemed as if Providence had His hand held out for protection and introduction. And why not? God upholds with the right hand of His righteousness, guides with His eye, is a sun and shield, and His attentions are most minute. The religious societies and the good companions were my safety and happiness.

It was an unspeakable good that I became a member of Mr. Paul's Bible class. I not only there received important religious instruction but found godly companions, and these introduced me to others who were a strength and comfort.

In my teens I became a member of the " Glasgow Young Men's Society for Religious Improvement." This society had many branches. The one I was connected with met in Wright's coffee-house, Trongate, every Sabbath morning at seven o'clock. The members in rotation presided. There were singing, prayer, reading of God's Word, questions asked and opinions freely given on the portion read. Once a month the members read essays, which were criticized. On week evenings there were frequent social gatherings which were times of much enjoyment. Hearts got knit, wits were sharpened, and many were the smiles that rested on the faces.

It is not too much to say that this Sabbath morning meeting was a Divinity hall ; and that from it many afterwards became ministers and missionaries, conspicuous philanthropists, and prince merchants. I was appointed secretary for the branch, and acted as such till I removed to England. On leaving there was a social gathering of the members, when they presented me with a handsome copy of Calmet's " Dictionary of the Holy Bible." It was not without much regret that I had to leave so many dear friends, but their memories, with recollections of the meetings, are ever present, spirit with spirit in fellowship, and by prayer gathering around the common mercy-seat.

As Mr. Nasmith may be considered the founder of these Young Men's Meetings, I think it right to make a brief reference to him. An extended life of him was written by the Rev. Dr. John Campbell, of London, and we are pleased to see a short account in the " Young Men's Christian Magazine." From the latter we make the following extract :—

" David Nasmith was born in the City of Glasgow, March 21, 1799. He was converted in early youth, and was soon distinguished by his energy of character and great zeal for the salvation of souls. Soon after his conversion, he with some school companions, formed the Glasgow Youth's Bible Association, and he became secretary of the organisation. About 1824 he became desirous of forming Young Men's Societies for religious improvement. To conceive with him was to execute, and we soon find him busily engaged in enlisting the labours of the first preachers of the age in their behalf. So indefatigable was he in his efforts that he travelled throughout the United Kingdom, France and America, establishing in these places about 70 Young Men's Societies. But, devoutly attached as he was to those societies, he had another great work pressing upon his heart—that of City Missions; and with these his name will go down to posterity. In 1826 (January 1) he formed the Glasgow City Mission. Similar societies were also formed in Dublin, Leith, and other cities.

" On the 27th July, 1830, he set sail from Greenock, Scotland, for New York, reaching there on 3rd September, and landing on the following day. On the 28th September he organised the New York City Mission. From that date he travelled forming City Missions and Young Men's Societies. In 30 days' visit to the south he formed six City Missions and six Young Men's Societies.

* * * * * *

"During the winter months of 1823, David Nasmith, everywhere he could, collected small companies of young men, strove to incite them to undertake some living work for their own improvement and the benefit of others. Kindled by his glowing enthusiasm, some like-minded young men rallied round him, formed a committee, considered the subject, banded themselves together, compacted their thoughts into shape, and formed a confederation for personal and spiritual training. On the morning of the New Year, 1824, David Nasmith had these young men with him to breakfast, along with some experienced Christian friends. Some time after they attended in a body, with their companions, a sermon which they had asked Dr. R. Wardlaw to preach to them, and then the public became aware that there had been instituted ' The Glasgow Young Men's Society for Religious Improvement '—the pioneer of the Young Men's Christian Association of the world."

Mr. Nasmith's life, after his return from America in December, 1831, continued such a restless one— a running to and fro, here and there and everywhere, seeking to do good—that we can do little more than chronicle the places and dates. Indeed, there were those who blamed him for such frequent absence from his family, and said that he should have been as Paul, *unmarried*, having no home ties and duties.   But he was justified in his own spirit, and his works praise him.

We find him visiting Boulogne, June 30, 1832; and before leaving the Continent he had the satisfaction of seeing at Paris a City Mission at work, with three agents.   On returning, he spent a short time in London, but it was not the opportune season for his work ; then he returns to Glasgow. In this city he prosecuted his labours with his usual energy, printing tracts, promoting revival meetings, young men's, tract, temperance, and other societies. But his operations were wider than his money means, and involved him in serious difficulties, when he is obliged to seek other ways for a livelihood. He next visits Ireland on behalf of the Continental Society.   Glasgow during this period was the centre of his operations.

Afterwards Mr. Nasmith settled in London, and succeeds in establishing a City Mission—an institution that has done and is doing untold good.   This was in the year 1835.   After two years, having severed his connection with this Society, he formed " The British and Foreign Mission, for the purpose of opening correspondence with all existing City and Town Missions, and planting new ones where they do not exist, to the extent of our ability, and by such other means as Divine Providence may point out, to do good to the souls and bodies of men."   This new Society was founded March 16, 1837; and, be it remembered, only three persons were present at its formation.   This trinity of persons were as the mustard seed that became the greatest of trees—a small beginning with mighty results. A Town and Young Men's Society were formed in Cambridge. He then proceeds to Ely and forms a Young Men's Society; then visits Birmingham and forms, in April, a Mission; then another at West Bromwich; and in the same month, on the 25th, there is the establishment of one at Manchester. Afterwards, in the same year, we find him at Leeds, Bradford, Halifax, Huddersfield, Wakefield, and York, establishing Town Missions and other Societies. He re-visits Scotland—"Falkirk, Glasgow, Paisley, Dumbarton, endeavouring by all practical means to do good, and advance the interests of the British and Foreign Mission."

The year 1838 opened upon David, surrounded with difficulties, but full of zeal for the glory of God and the good of mankind. The first Sabbath of the year drew forth the following reflections: " I am on my journey to heaven; I am more than three-quarters past my thirty-eighth milestone on the road, and soon shall be at the thirty-ninth milestone. To mark progress is wisdom; to pass on without consideration is folly. Let *me* be wise, be fools who may! Had I been more wise, I should have been more happy this day, and the world would have been more blessed on my account. Great usefulness is my aim: let it not be my idol. Great holiness is my aim: let me enjoy, but not *glory* in anything but Christ. . . ."

The same year we find Mr. Nasmith in Wales, in Dublin; returns to England, visits Oxford and other towns; at each place full of work for Jesus, but throughout the length and breadth of the land, hampered for want of means. His diary of September 6, 1839, runs thus : "For several days I have been in great agony of spirit from want of money. I had given my wife, at the close of last week, every fraction of money in my possession, so that I have not had one halfpenny in my pocket; and my dear wife has had her trial of faith, anxious with myself to pay every man, and not being at all inclined to have people asking for money when due, without the power of giving it. We have both been several times in prayer, but the answer is delayed. Our faith is put to the test. . . ."

The end of this remarkable life nears. Mr. Nasmith visits Guildford to endeavour to form a Town Mission. When calling on one of the friends, he complained of "feeling considerable pain at his chest. The pain continued there for a minute or two, and then removed to his bowels, where it raged with most excruciating agony." Becoming helpless, a carriage was procured, and he was removed to an inn, where medical advice was immediately procured. Notwithstanding his agony of pain, his Christian spirit was victor. A friend said, "It is hard, amidst such troubles as these, to say, 'The Lord's will be done.'" But he replied, with much energy, "NOT AT ALL." Many joyous expressions were uttered during his last hours. One was, "On hearing the church bells, he said, 'Do the tribes of the Lord go up to-day? Oh! this is sent to humble me and to prove me. Oh! the rapture of that time when I shall cast my blood-bought crown at my Redeemer's feet!'" He died November 17, 1839, only forty years old; yet what a life of noble results!

Mr. Paul, being called to leave Glasgow to be a missionary in connection with a congregational church in Yorkshire, I was asked to be his successor in the Sabbath school. This I at first refused; Mr. Paul being one of the best of teachers—apt and fluent in speech, full of rich humour, attractive in delivery, having a wide knowledge of the Scriptures and of men and things,—I felt altogether unfitted to succeed him. I had not sufficient Bible knowledge, or experience, or readiness in utterance; was timid, and only about 19 years old. He would not accept my refusal, but urgently pressed the question, saying some such words—" Make the trial; do your best; trust in God, and He will help you." At last I yielded and became the teacher. By Divine help I was somewhat successful, but never could take Mr. Paul's place fully, either for tact or efficiency.

I would fail in duty if there were no further notice of the invaluable life of Mr. Paul. He was a remarkable man—full of exuberant buoyance all through life, and ever ready for his Master's work. I never met with a Christian that had such a mixture of the gay and the grave—the sunshine of company chastened with religious awe. On one occasion Mr. Paul was called to address a social meeting at Bradford. Many were gathered together, and it was a time for smiles and words of good cheer. He commenced his speech in some such

words as the following:—"Mr. Chairman and dear
Christian friends, I am sorry to say"—and there
was much apparent sadness in the lines of the face
and the intonation of the voice—"that I have lost
this day two invaluable friends that have been with
me all through life—faithful servants at all times, but
this day we have been for ever separated, and now I
have to lament their loss."   There was sympathetic
tension in the meeting—all ready with their con-
dolence, but imagine their rebound of feeling, when
he told them that the two friends he had lost were
two teeth that the dentist had extracted.   There was
merry laughter all around.   Afterwards he delivered
an interesting speech.   This was like the man—
playful as a child and serious as a sage.   Mr. Paul
became minister of the Independent church at
Wibsey—yea, the church owed its existence to his
unwearied successful efforts.   The following is from
an "Address delivered on Tuesday, the 29th May,
1860, over the body of the Rev. John Paul, minister
of the Independent Chapel, Wibsey, by James R.
Campbell, M.A., minister of Horton Lane Chapel,
Bradford:—"

"Our friend died when he was sixty-three years old.

"For sixty of these years he may be said to have
been under the sensible influences of Christian truth.
He fondly remembered and recounted that he was
a child of three years, when (as Samuel in the hand of
Hannah) he was taken by his pious mother to hear
one of the greatest and most successful preachers of
his time, the late Greville Ewing, of Glasgow, his
mother's and his own pastor.

"It was a time of great religious quickening in those parts. Under the force of that quickening, this gifted minister of Christ, Mr. Ewing, broke from the restraints of the Established Church, of which he had been a distinguished ornament, and gave himself to street preaching, to field preaching, and to preaching in every place in which he could gather sinners to hear the joyful sound. Amongst the thousands who were streaming daily to hear this great and good man, a man of almost angelic aspect, and extraordinary eloquence, was this mother with her child of three years old in her hand. It may be that on that very day, which he so distinctly remembered, the purpose and prayer of that godly woman fixed the direction and habit of John Paul's religious thoughts, as he drank into his soul of childhood some of that hallowed enthusiasm which was burning in his mother's bosom.

"It was not till 1815—fifteen years afterwards—that he took his place among the openly avowed disciples of Christ. He was afterwards chosen a deacon of the same church.

"His Christianity must even then have been of a strong and energetic type; for, not long after, avowing himself a disciple of Christ, we find him pursuing the steps of his Divine Master, in lifting the degraded and outcast into the dignity of children of God. There is no local similitude by means of which I might describe to you 'The Goose Dubs,' the scene of his early and long-continued labours for Christ. The hiding-place rather than the habitation of the most degraded and reckless in the City of

Glasgow,* it was there that for fifteen years he breathed the damp, pestilential vapour of the low-roofed, ill-ventilated rooms into which he gathered the children of his Sabbath school, and men and women, whom in his first efforts as a preacher, he sought to convert from the error of their ways.

"I do not forget the excellent example and faithful lessons of that pious mother, of whom he spoke with a pleasing simplicity of veneration as if he were still the boy looking up in her face—I as little forget the singularly rich expositions of Divine truth to which he listened, in his regular attendance upon Mr. Ewing's ministry—but I say that the 'Goose Dubs' of Glasgow was the college in which

---

* Mr. Forbes, of Milligan, Forbes, & Co., thus describes his first sight of "The Goose Dubs," and of the friend betwixt whom and himself there was that night formed an unalterable affection :—

"I cannot describe the sensation I experienced at the scenes I witnessed in passing along the 'Dubs.' At length we came to a large tumble-down, shed-like sort of erection. We ascended some most dilapidated stone steps, and in the place was assembled a large number of men and women in the most wretched ragged state I ever beheld human beings. Mr. Paul had not arrived, but we were received by a female—his coadjutor at his religious meetings in that locality. Her services in that capacity were invaluable. She had been one of the vilest in Glasgow, wallowing in every kind of sin. Under the preaching of dear Paul she was brought to Christ, and became a most eminent Christian. So much so—such was her love to Christ—such her devoted efforts for the promotion of His glory, and for winning souls to Christ, that at her death, which occurred after Paul came to Bradford her remains were followed to the grave by Dr. Wardlaw, Mr. Ewing, and a large number of Christian friends, who bewailed the loss of her Christian services."

Mr. Paul was trained for the ministry in these parts. He had not then and he never afterwards put on the complete armour of the trained man of war, for he had not proved it. But his sling when thrown in the name of the Mighty God, he had proved in the 'Goose Dubs.' As he had triumphed in Christ there, he hoped to succeed by the same weapon when he came among you. And he was not disappointed.

"Even while yet following a secular calling, he was, in the preaching of the glorious Gospel, a workman that needed not to be ashamed.

"It was not till he came to Bradford in 1834 that he gave himself wholly to the labours of an evangelist and minister of the Gospel. . . . To his work he zealously devoted himself from the very first—in Bradford, and Little Horton, and Wibsey together, until, in process of time, Wibsey absorbed all his energies. What he was then, he was to the end—a man of honest, manly, straightforward purpose; not seeking, or pretending to high things, but heartily loving true real things; a neighbourly upright benevolent Christian man in the pulpit and out of it.

"The fact that considerable numbers regularly waited on his preaching in the old schoolroom, and that some of them had experienced a saving change, and had united themselves with the church in Horton Lane, suggested and justified the attempt to form a Congregational Church in this place.

"Seven years from the time that Mr. Paul came to Bradford, that is in 1841, this chapel was opened for the worship of God, and in the year following (1842) the church was formed.

*   *   *   *   *   *

"It was not for a year after the church was formed that the system of ministerial supplies was superseded by an invitation of the church (concurred in by the congregation) to Mr. Paul to take the pastoral office.   To this he was ordained in 1843.

"From that day to this he has lived in all good conscience before you and among you.   His attachment to this place and this people was strong and openly avowed.   It was literally in his heart to die and to live with you.

"When failing health suggested his retirement from the pastorate, it was your interests, and not his own ease or gratification, which prompted the act.

"Accordingly, when you fitly and gracefully declined to receive his resignation, he would not yield himself to the seducement of this highly-valued kindness on your part, but persisted in a purpose which he believed was for the true welfare of this church and of this village.

*   *   *   *   *   *

"The last time he was in this chapel was in January of this year.   He was feeble, and the hospitality of devoted friends induced him to try a change.   But the hand of death was upon him; he must go home.   It was his peremptory wish.   If he must die, he would meet the last enemy on the spot on which he had often magnified the Divine Conqueror of death."

When there was read to him that part of the 23rd Psalm, in which God promises to be with His people when walking through the valley and shadow of death, he said, in his firm emphatic way, "AY! THAT IS IT." The day before he died, he was asked if Christ was precious and felt to "be sufficient." His answer was, "I REJOICE IN HIM." His last audible words were, "TELL THE CHURCH I LOVE THEM." This was the dying legacy of a faithful minister.

Besides being engaged in Sabbath school work, two or three of s went together on Sabbath forenoons to one or her of the hamlets outside of the city to circulate acts and hold address meetings. We generally fod a readiness on the part of the people to open the houses for a religious service, and the tracts were thankfully received. With weakness and imperfection Jesus and His salvation were offered to the people, and scattering the indestructible seed of the kingdom, good must have been done.

One of my most faithful associates in this work was Mr. William Finlayson. We were to each other as "Jonathan and David." Many were our walks of usefulness; but these were to terminate. My friend went to Australia, hoping to be a missionary amongst the aborigines. When he and his wife landed—some fifty years ago—there was no house, and a temporary one had to be made. Four posts in a square were fixed in the ground, around which blankets were fastened. In this primitive booth we have been told his wife gave birth to her first-born.

The mission to the aborigines had to be abandoned, and attention was given to the settlers. God blessed the effort. Mr. F. succeeded in gathering a congregation. Souls were converted and formed into a church, when he was chosen pastor. For many years he has ministered the word, and not a few can speak of him as their spiritual father. His dear wife, full of years and good work, died October 20, 1884, aged 73 years. They might well put on her memorial card: " Her children arise and call her blessed : her husband also, and he praiseth her" (Prov. xxxi. 28). The husband, though surrounded by the loving attentions of his children, feels her loss, and patiently waits the coming of Jesus, when there will be happy re-union.

In connection with the above we give the following extract from the *S. A. Register*, October 25, 1884 :—" We have to record the death of one of the earliest colonists, Mrs. William Finlayson, of Helenholme, near Mitcham. With her husband she arrived in South Australia, in 'The John Renwick,' in February 1837, some six weeks after the proclamation of the colony. These were, indeed, primitive times, and the hardships which the young couple had to endure in common with the few score other persons who had then reached these shores, were neither few nor small. All their privations and troubles were, however, borne with a fortitude and hopefulness which some immigrants of more recent days have failed to emulate. Mr. Finlayson came out with the idea of acting as a missionary to the natives, but he was unable to carry out his design except to a very modified extent. Entering the employ of the South Australian Company, he and his wife took up their quarters a few miles from Adelaide, and often, in the absence of her husband, whose name is to be found on the list of the early explorers, Mrs. Finlayson found herself alone with hundreds of savages, who, however, never attempted to molest her, but treated her with profound respect, and submitted themselves implicitly to her directions. Not long after coming to the colony, Mr. and Mrs. Finlayson settled on a farm near Mitcham, to which the name of Helenholme was given, where they continued for something like a quarter of a century. As their children grew up the parents removed to Adelaide, but three or four years ago they returned to their former residence. The deceased lady studiously avoided taking part in public movements, but much of her time was devoted to deeds of kindness and charity. Her motto throughout life was, 'Better are the blessings of the poor than the praises of the rich,' and scores of those who have been the recipients of her kindly counsel and generous help affectionately cherish her memory, and will genuinely mourn the death of one ever ready with consolation and succour. Mrs. Finlayson had reached her 73rd year when she fell a victim to an illness beginning with inflammation of the lungs, which had kept her a prisoner for five months. She leaves behind—her husband, four sons (Messrs. R. K. Finlayson, W. Finlayson, J. Harvey Finlayson, and E. Finlayson), five daughters, and 24 grand-children."

On Sabbath evenings, at eight o'clock, it was my privilege to have an Address Meeting in that wretched district the Old Wynd. Here, too, attention by the people was given to God's Word. I had, besides, a district in connection with the Monthly Tract Society. A short account of this Society is given in second number of the *Christian Philanthropist's Companion* :—

"A Society was formed in Glasgow, on the 13th of March last year [1832], for the purpose of leaving a tract monthly at every house in the city and its vicinity, and a copy of the same tract with all. The first issues were made in July following, and amounted that month to 15,839. Up to the end of the year, 111,167 tracts had been issued by the hands of 493 distributors; of these distributors upwards of one-fifth were females. The average refusal of tracts was one in 120. During the present year the distributors and the issues have been somewhat increased. The issues are now about 30,000 monthly, and the distributors about 600."

CHAPTER VI.

A Church Member.

"The Church of the living God, the pillar and ground of the truth."—1 TIM. iii. 15.

"Lord, 'tis a pleasant thing to stand
In gardens planted by Thy hand;
Let me within Thine courts be seen,
Like a young cedar fresh and green."

WATTS.

DURING the first five or six years of our residence in Glasgow I attended, with my parents, the United Presbyterian Church, Eglinton Street, then favoured with the ministrations of the Rev. John Johnson. He was considered one of the finest readers and orators in the city. Although I somewhat enjoyed his preaching, it did not impress me as much as I desired. This was the period in my history when I strove after acquiring painful experience, thinking it essential for salvation. My wish was that the minister's words should go deep into the soul and produce broken-heartedness. Generally I left the service disappointed, not feeling anguish of mind. The preaching, however, was a good for which I desire to thank God. Two or three of his sermons on the Transfiguration of Christ have left but a hazy impression. In the Transfiguration there is so much favourable for word-painting, that Mr. Johnson's dramatic powers had full scope. His words, intonation, and action, impressed me, and the sense of the impression lives in the memory.

I attended a Bible-class which Mr. Johnson held in the Session-house. He sat at the head of a long table, with the members of the class on his right and left. The Bible lay open before him, a silver pencil-case was in his hand, and he spoke instructive words with kindliness. There were reading, questions put and answered, remarks on and the enforcement of the subject, all tending to profit and to knit the hearts of the young to their minister.

Connected with the church were choice spirits, of whom some were conspicuous for practical goodness, were men of prayer, of purity, of benevolence, and ever ready for Christian work. Three of these relinquished their membership in the U. P. Church and joined the Baptist denomination. This change of opinion excited my curiosity, and led me to inquiry on the subject of Christian baptism. Not having any books on the question, I sent an anonymous letter to the Rev. Dr. Paterson, Baptist minister, asking for his views. It was signed, " An Inquirer." A kind answer was received, recommending me to read the New Testament on the subject, and offering, if desired, a personal interview. I also asked the advice of one of the persons who had left Mr. Johnson's church. He gave me Cruden's " Concordance," urging a careful examination of all the passages on baptism and circumcision. The result of this study was that I accepted the

Baptists' views. On the night of my baptism, Robert Kettle, Esq., the Christian philanthropist, and Agnes Gray, who afterwards became my wife, were also baptized. Many gathered together to see the "strange sight;" and, personally, I bless God for the privilege of being "buried with Christ in baptism."

A remarkable incident may be mentioned. Dr. Paterson, after receiving the note from "An Inquirer," mentioned the circumstance at a Church Meeting, saying, that having had such a letter, he thought it his duty to answer it by preaching a course of discourses on baptism. This he did; but on the very night of the first discourse "Inquirer" was baptized. When the Doctor was apprised of the fact, he gave one of his hearty laughs.

The Baptist Congregation at this time met in the Rev. Dr. Dick's old church, Inklefactory Lane. The gallery, which was floored off from the lower part, only was used. It made a convenient meeting place, and would seat three or four hundred persons. Many hallowed seasons were spent in it.

After a few years, when I was still a member of the church, a new chapel was built in Hope Street. Dr. Paterson's able and faithful ministrations were much blessed in conversion and edification. Beginning his pastorate with a very few members the church increased to two or three hundred.

The Doctor's preaching, although not popular in style, was full of conviction and instruction. He was a *conscience* preacher—grappled with doubt and the sinner's excuses. His Wednesday evening's discourses were free-and-easy; without any manuscript, and as a rule were much enjoyed. He, too, was a faithful pastor, caring for his flock; ever ready to visit the afflicted and sorrowing. His ministrations in the "house of mourning" were appropriate and sympathetic, and his prayers carried the soul near to Jesus and the fulness of His grace. The "lambs" were not overlooked, for them he had a Bible class which was much valued. Besides, the Doctor had a secular class for the benefit of a few young men, of which I was a member. He gave us lessons in Greek, adopting the interlinear system. I have reason to bless God for his teachings.

The Doctor is dead, but his labours live, and the congregation now worship in a handsome church in Adelaide Place. Few of the early members survive, but there are the "children and the children's children" that have arisen to call God blessed. We well remember the "day of small things," and now bless God that, in a sense, the "little one has become a thousand."

Although my views were changed on the subject of baptism, I have not lost my strong affection for the church of my fathers. Never, while memory lives and reason retains its seat, can I forget the United Presbyterian Church, and it is still a privilege to have occasionally fellowship with her members.

"Peace be within thy walls, and prosperity within thy palaces. For my brethren and companions' sakes, I will now say, Peace be within thee. Because of the house of the Lord our God I will seek thy good."

CHAPTER VII.

A Missionary.

" He seems no stranger in that poor abode ;
    Nor be he strange, he tells them of their God.
    Yet sure he seems unequal to the task ;
    Such rugged labours more experience ask,
    Scarce twice ten years have marked his thoughtful face,
    And dares he mingle with that stubborn race?"

WILLIAM THOMSON.

DURING the first years of my religious life I had great fondness for mission literature. The lives of missionaries were especially interesting. I remember being greatly pleased when a compositor, to put into type intelligence from missionaries in Africa connected with the Glasgow Missionary Society. The experiences of the native converts made the heart glow. Full of interest to me also were missionary meetings which I was sure to attend when opportunity offered.

When about twenty years old I had a strong desire to be employed as a *Mission printer*. This desire was greatly strengthened by the visit of the Rev. John Williams, missionary, from the South Seas. Numerous meetings attended by large numbers were held, and intensely popular addresses

which greatly moved the heart were given. I had
an interview with Mr. Williams, and opened my
mind to him. He much encouraged the desire, and
expressed willingness that I should accompany him
on his return. Some time after the directors of the
London Missionary Society were informed of this
interview, and when the time neared for the
missionary's return, I was asked to prepare for
leaving. Up to this time the directors were not
aware that I was a Baptist, though the fact had
been stated to Mr. Williams. When it became
known, the secretary wrote that it was contrary to
the Society's rules to send an " anti-pædobaptist "
to any of their stations.

Expectations and hopes being disappointed as to
Foreign Missions, my attention was called in 1837
to an advertisement in the *Patriot* newspaper for
Town Missionaries for Manchester. I wrote the
secretary asking for particulars as to work, etc.
Instead of having my questions answered, I was
asked to meet the directors at their office. I did so,
and was at once engaged. A short time before this,
I was married to a Christian lady who was actively
engaged in philanthropic work. We removed to
England, and took with us her two orphan nieces.

The district to which I was appointed was dark
and benighted—one part largely occupied by
Romanists. The duties were:—visitation from house
to house with tracts, religious converse, reading and
prayer when convenient, and holding address meetings in the district. This interesting work was
continued for more than a year. I had kindly

receptions of the people, several professing a change of heart and life.

One fact the directors kept from me which I learned afterwards, namely, that my predecessor had in one part of the district excited the ire of the Romanists by attacking their system, and they would not hear him, but chased him from their street, throwing stones after him. It was my rule when visiting Roman Catholic families, after kindly inquiring for their welfare, to ask if they had a Prayer book, and receiving it, to read one of the penitential psalms, enforcing the truth there taught. In this way confidence and a hearing were gained. In no instance was I rudely treated.

A circumstance happened in my district that somewhat modified my views about Town Missions. A poor widow was converted. She was naturally intelligent, and gave much attention to the study of God's Word. Having given herself to Christ, she had a desire to give herself to God's people, and she naturally looked to her missionary for guidance. She knew nothing about the differences that separated Christians ; and with the simplicity of a child asked for instruction. But her questions had to be evaded. Somewhat grieved in spirit, one forenoon she thus addressed the missionary : " Mr. ———, have you heard of that case of drowning?" " No," was the reply. " Well, a person was nearly drowned—sinking in the water—when an expert swimmer saved her ; but, instead of conveying her to a house of safety, where she would be cared for, laid her down by the water side. What do you think of his conduct ?"

E

"Oh," said the missionary, "I think he ought to have been more careful, and taken her to a house." "Well," said she, "thou art the man. You have been the means of saving me from drowning in the pit of perdition; but, instead of conveying me to a proper church, you have left me to myself; and I know not what to do." The missionary was in a dilemma, and had to explain that the rules of the mission would not admit of giving advice on such matters. She was then asked to go to God in earnest prayer; tell Him her case; read God's Word with attention; and the Spirit would become her guide. This fact led the missionary to feel that by being *thus* tied by human rules, he was violating the words of Jesus, which say "Teaching them to observe all things, whatsoever I have commanded you."

Doubtless missions are a great good in our towns and cities. Hundreds have been converted, and made trophies of the wondrous love of Jesus. Many have been their temporal and spiritual blessings. And it is a pleasing sight to see Christians of varied denominations combining for the spiritual good of their fellow creatures. But could not these benefits follow *generous* action to the missionary, allowing him in special cases to teach what he conceives the whole will of God? Proselytizing may well be detested: we abhor the conduct of that man who would be more zealous to bring over persons to a party than to Christ; still there are cases when advice ought to be given.

Isaac Crewdson, Esq., who left the old body of the Quakers and formed what may be called a new sect,* was my superintendent. He was one of the directors of the mission, and was an eminently good man. It was a privilege to meet him, as I frequently did, at his own house to tea, and to receive his wise counsels. Few men physically had a finer make, or morally had more attractive power. He was a magnet of goodness. When he left the old body of Quakers, he published "The Trumpet Blown," which contained an account of his religious views. He also printed, principally for gratuitous circulation, Baxter's "Saints' Rest" and Fuller on "Religious Declension." A copy of each he gave me, writing on them my name with his Christian regards. I bless God for the fellowships of this holy man, and revere his memory!

While living in Manchester, prizes were offered for the best essay on "The Duty of the Church to Support Christian Missions." The first prize was won by the Rev. Dr. Harris, who adopted as his title, "Mammon." The subject of Missions being congenial, I devoted spare time to writing on it, having no idea of publication. The manuscript when finished was read by an evangelical friend, a gentleman who had shown me much kindness, and who urged its publication, saying he would run all money risk. After examination, an eminent minister

---

* This sect, called "Evangelical Friends," only existed a few years. During Mr. Crewdson's time, who was the principal minister, a chapel was built in Grosvenor Street, Manchester, where the "Friends" and families met for worship. Shortly after Mr. Crewdson's death the congregation got scattered, and the chapel was sold.

of Manchester offered to write an introductory chapter. The book when published was well received. Favourable notices appeared in the *Eclectic Review* and other magazines. Its title was "Christian Missions: comprising an Account of the Moral State of the World."

At the same time was printed a pamphlet headed "Glory Departed: being an Address to British Churches." The design of the writer was to urge on churches oneness, love, zeal, and prayer—duties he considered in a large measure lacking; and for want of them the glory of the Pentecostal era had departed.

"For Zion's sake will I not hold my peace, and for Jerusalem's sake I will not rest, until the righteousness thereof go forth as brightness and the salvation thereof as a lamp that burneth. And the Gentiles shall see thy righteousness, and all kings thy glory: and thou shalt be called by a new name, which the mouth of the Lord shall name."

CHAPTER VIII.

𝔄 Pastor.

"For though I preach the Gospel, I have nothing to glory of : for necessity is laid upon ; yea, woe is unto me, if I preach not the Gospel."—1 Cor. ix. 16.

"A divine ought to calculate his sermon, as an astronomer does his almanac, to the meridian of the place and people where he lives."—Palmer.

WHATEVER my ambition I never aspired to be a minister. The office was too dignified in importance, in learning and in sacredness. In my teens I was awed by the presence and converse of clergymen ; but to be one of them was an honour to which I did not then look forward. I felt willing to serve God in an humble way, as a printer at a mission station, and talk for Jesus as leisure and opportunity offered. The ministry was unsought and came unexpected. In a sense I was thrust into the office.

An eminent Christian minister of Bolton waited on me ; having had no previous notice, his visit was a surprise. His mission was to know if I would go to a populous village some ten miles distant from Manchester, and there labour under the auspices of the Lancashire and Cheshire Association. The village had a population of about 4000 with only three places of worship—the Church of England, a Unitarian meeting-house, and a small Baptist chapel. It was proverbial for its cruel sports, its infidelity, and its wickedness. It was sometimes called "the back settlements of *England*." Several *unsuccessful* attempts to establish religious interests led the Unitarians to boast of their hold of the place. Such a village, next to going to a heathen land, was congenial, and I readily accepted the offer considering it as a call from God. Relinquishing my connection with the Manchester Town Mission, I removed to this village in the year 1839.

At first there was much to discourage. There were only about seven Baptists in the district—four in the village, a very small congregation and school, and no preaching in the forenoon. At 11 o'clock there was a catechetical service, attended by a few adults and the scholars; in the afternoon the children were taught, and at night there was preaching; after which a prayer-meeting was held.

God smiled on the effort. After a few weeks the congregation so increased that there was preaching in the morning. The catechetical service, being appreciated, was held in the afternoon, at the close of teaching, from three to four o'clock. Souls were converted and a church formed, of which I became pastor. Some of the persons converted had been noted for infidelity, cruel sports, and open wickedness. One of the converts had shown his enmity to the Bible by burning it at the Cross. This person was very impressive in prayer: he seemed as under a huge stone, burdened by a sense of guilt, groaning out his petitions before God with many tears. When about to give up the ghost, he tried to sing the hymn,

" There is a fountain filled with blood," etc.

Cottage services, meeting in different parts of the village, were well attended and largely blessed. One of them was held in the house of the converted infidel, in a place called Limbo—mouth of hell— next door to the noted bull-baiter. We considered it our duty to wait on the leader in this wild sport. He received us kindly, and the excuse he urged was : " The rich people have their horse-racing and hunting, why should not the poor have their bull-baiting ?" I am thankful to say that this barbarous sport was stopped in a year or two afterwards.

Three years had not passed before it was considered expedient to have a new chapel. The opinion of the committee of the Association was asked, and they encouraged the undertaking. Monetary responsibilities rested on myself, but I was greatly relieved by the generous munificence of certain gentlemen who gave large sums towards the building. The rare action of George Foster, Esq., of Sabden, must not be overlooked. He not only contributed largely, but generously placed at my disposal a princely sum to meet the bills as they fell due.

I left home for about three months on a collecting tour ; visited Scotland—not overlooking the Highlands—and can never forget the kindness of the people everywhere. By God's goodness a handsome sum was raised.

I well remember the Sabbath spent at Blair Athol, where I preached, and where an old lady favoured me with the "kiss of charity;" and also the Sabbath spent at Grantown with the good Peter Grant. He asked if I was prepared to give them a two hours' sermon; saying that they had one service, that many of the people had come ten and more miles, and that they liked good measure? I replied, that I had no sermon of that length, but would preach two if desired. It was arranged that I should preach a sermon in English, and that Mr. Grant should preach one in Gaelic. There was a large congregation, eager attention, and a little enthusiasm when listening to the eloquent words of their own minister. In the harvest of the world the results of this day's labours will be known.

The name given to the chapel was "Hephzibah," expressive of my deep interest in it. When opened by the Rev. C. M. Birrell, of Liverpool, he took for his text, "Thou shalt be called Hephzibah" (Isaiah lxii. 4). It was an impressive discourse, and very suitable for the occasion. In the afternoon a sermon was preached by the Rev. W. F. Barchell, of Rochdale; and in the evening a public meeting was held, when addresses were given by ministers and others. On the Sabbath after the pulpit was occupied by the Rev. John Paul, of Wibsey, near Bradford.

The "opening" was a day of glad memories. Many kind friends came from a distance, and showed their interest not only by their presence, but by their generous offerings. All were thankful for what God had done in a village that had been *so* given over to the wicked one.

The Unitarian chapel originally belonged to the Presbyterians. Report said that Matthew Henry, the Commentator, had preached in it. *Sad that there should have been such a change!* SAD, that where the Bible had been received as the inspired Word of God, the only rule of faith and practice, it should *now* be considered as an imperfect book, subject to reason "falsely so called." SAD, that where Christ was exalted "over all, God blessed for ever," a true object of worship, He should *now* be made only a man, with an imperfect nature. SAD, that where Jesus' death was taught as the one only Sacrificial Offering for sin, it should *now* be ranked amongst martyrdoms for the truth. And, SAD, that where faith in the Person and Work of Jesus was preached as the one way of eternal life, a system of morality should *now* be substituted. Alas! "Ichabod!" where is the glory?

The Unitarian congregation was numerous and influential; and minister and people were zealous in teaching their principles. They not only sought to retain their standing, but were anxious to widen it. A course of lectures was annually delivered by popular preachers; and to give variety and interest, each preacher took one of the course. These excited attention, and persons for miles round attended them.

For three years I gave attention to simply preaching the Gospel, which God blessed in the conversion of sinners. *Now* that there were many young people in the church and congregation, I thought it right to seek their establishment in the truth of Christ's Deity. Six discourses on the subject were announced and delivered. These excited attention, and drew together large congregations; amongst the number many Unitarians, sometimes their minister.

After the delivery of the discourses, I was asked to publish them. This was partly declined, but an abridgment was printed, under the title, " Berea; or, A Scriptural Manual on the Doctrine of a Triune God." This small sixpenny book was considered worthy of a ninepenny review by Rev. Dr. ———, the Unitarian minister!

In answer to the review I printed a pamphlet, entitled, " The Reviewer Examined," etc. When " The Reviewer Examined " was issued, many of the Unitarians felt dissatisfied, and asked the Doctor to answer the " Strictures." He said, " I will not print any more, but will answer them by a lecture." This he did on a Sabbath eve—most inconvenient for me, as I ought then to be preaching in my own chapel. However, I secured a supply and went to hear the Doctor's answer. There was a large congregation, and my presence attracted notice.

At the close of the lecture I met the Doctor at the foot of the pulpit-stairs, and asked, after shaking hands, " Are you going to print your lecture ? " " No," was the reply; " I have done with printing." " Well, Doctor, what am I to do ? You had my pamphlet with you in your study, and could reply perfectly. I have only short notes of your lecture;

will you favour me with your manuscript?" "You will not be able to make anything of it; it is in shorthand, and I have a system of mine own." "Well, Doctor, that being the case, will you favour me with a copy in plain hand?" "I will think over it, and let you know in the morning."

On the morrow a short note was received, declining to give a copy.

Having taken notes of the lecture, I replied as perfectly as I could, sending the Doctor an invitation to the meeting, which he did not accept. In a large congregation many Unitarians were present. Thus ended a controversy which was supposed to have done much good.

Notwithstanding this war of words the Unitarian minister and myself continued friends. A short time afterwards we met in the house of a sick person, when he read a chapter, without comment, and I prayed. On leaving—while standing together in the street—he said, "Mr. ———, I think you have hard views of me. I am not a Socinian." "Oh, no, Doctor, you are an Arian; and you do not believe in Christ's sacrificial, vicarious character." He made no reply, and we separated after shaking hands.

There is one pleasing incident connected with the "Berea" which may gratefully be recorded. The Rev. C. M. Birrell said, "I so value the little book that it has a place with others I give on loan to inquirers and young converts."

A Revival Union, composed of those members of the church who were deeply interested in the work of conversion, had rich blessing. The names of persons for whom special interest was felt were mentioned, and written down in a book, and the members met weekly to pray for their conversion. One member after another on bended knee besought the Lord—laying the names and cases before Him. There was great urgency—some would plead with tears, that they might be saved. Each member of the Union was also furnished with a list of persons that he might daily spread it before God, as Hezekiah did the letter. Not satisfied with prayer, *direct* effort was used for their salvation—by conversation, tracts, and books. Remarkable to say, —is it remarkable, having such a faithful God who hears and answers prayer?—nearly all, if not all, were brought to a knowledge of the truth. It was interesting to look at the list with the names of those who had decided crossed off. Ah! "praying breath is never spent in vain."

Many of the members of the church and congregation were warm friends of temperance, some of whom were reclaimed drunkards, who had much reason to bless God for the benefit of total abstinence; others took the pledge—giving their name and influence—as examples to others. There was a flourishing society, and meetings were frequently held, occasionally addressed by some of the *first* advocates from Preston. It was my duty and privilege to give occasional lectures; four of which were printed by request, under the title, "Scriptural Union; or, Temperance Societies based on Bible principles." The pamphlet was published at the end of 1840 by Mr. J. Pasco, London. We give part of the preface :—"Among the many noble Institutions that are the glory of the age, we hail the Temperance Society as one of no mean nature. It is destined to act as Christ's *harbinger*, preparing the way for His spiritual reign, by removing mountains and hills. Although young in years, yet not to be despised ; for its strength daily increases, and ere long through the power of its might and the strength of its arm—guided and directed by Him with whom all things are possible—the world shall be shaken and the kingdom of darkness fall. We regard intemperance as the strongest pillar to the domains of Satan, so that when this institution becomes potent, it will seize the column, and Samson-like destroy the Philistines."

My dear wife under God was a great good in the village. She was incessant in her Christian efforts. The houses she freely visited, leaving tracts and having conversation with the people. She conducted a maternal meeting that was greatly enjoyed by the mothers ; had a large female Bible class (many of whom joined the church) ; and "in season and out of season" worked for Jesus. Even when health failed, she would not abate effort. The doctor saw that she was physically wasting, and must soon die if she continued in the cold, damp North, and urged a removal to the sunny South. Providence, ever wise and good, opened up a way at the nick of time. Of the four invitations to different churches then received, the one from a town of lovely Devonshire was considered most suitable for my wife.

In a small chapel, in an out-station in a hamlet two miles distant, were held a Sabbath school and preaching.   The village had a singular, ominous name, that sounded "dangerous," filled a small "corner" in God's great universe, was dark and be-nighted, and had little encouragement for Christian workers.   Still some good was done, and our hope is that it may yet become a well-watered Gospel corner.

This pastorate lasted seven years.   Never can I forget the pain of parting.   The church numbered about eighty, in a sense my spiritual children begotten by the Gospel.   Knit to every tendril of the heart, separation from them was a wrench that has never been healed.

This chapter would be incomplete if we did not refer to five members of the church.   The first was one of the seven Baptists I found in the district on settling.   He kept the ember-spark alive when there was no pastor.   Although living about three miles from the chapel, he was ever in his place, and was useful as a preacher and full of temperance zeal.   Night after night he would leave his home to attend a lecture, a prayer or a temperance meeting. He was an acceptable speaker, full of action, and his services were sought for miles round, so that his usefulness was widespread.   During my pastorate he removed to Yorkshire.   Afterwards he and his family emigrated to America.   He is now dead; but his works have followed him.

The second member, one of the early converts, was a young man.   On his decision for Christ, religion seemed to take hold of his entire self. It was not half work but full work for Jesus—body, soul, and spirit. In a sense he was a seraph. He could not do with a "frigid zone" profession, even a "temperate zone" one was scarcely tolerated; there must be "*torrid zone*" Christianity. He would beseech sinners with tears to be reconciled to God. At prayer and other meetings he was, in a measure, their interest and life. Oh, how he sang God's praise! with what urgency he prayed! Truly he had "power with God, and prevailed." He died early; but his short religious life was an expression that can never die.

The third member had a remarkable conversion. On a Sabbath eve, at the close of a sermon on blind Bartimeus, Jesus was represented as passing by, ready and anxious to save, and He might never again return. Sinners were urged to adopt the cry, "Jesus, thou Son of David, have mercy on me." This person was so deeply moved that he could not restrain himself, but fell down on his knees, and in deepest anguish sobbed aloud. He would have mercy *now*, and earnestly sought it. After service he came down to our house full of excitement. Words of instruction were given and prayer offered. Thank God! he found peace, and became one of the most active members of the church. He had a restless spirit, was excitable, a little peculiar, yet full of zeal. Religion to him was a reality, and doing good the business of his life. When first converted, such was his passion to win souls to Christ, he desired to relinquish business and give

himself entirely to this work; but he was told that
he could serve Jesus and be useful without this
sacrifice. He could win the affection of children
and talk attractively to them; his prayers brought
us nearer to God, and had the effect of Jacob's
wrestlings. In many ways he served the church.
Years after I left he continued his membership; but
afterwards, for some cause, withdrew, but not from
Christian action; for even now he lives to carry on
important work in connection with a "Mission
Hall, Ragged School, and Refuge for the Destitute."
We are informed he has "gathered from the streets
over a thousand ragged children; that some are
saved and doing well, some in heaven, and some safe
for heaven." Also, that he has "persuaded some
thousands of young and old to become total
abstainers." We wish him God-speed in all good
work !

The fourth member had distinctive marks. Up
to the age of twenty-five he was regardless of religion,
and spent his Sabbaths either idly at home, or
abroad in the fields. A tract given him, awakened
his attention, made him thoughtful, and caused him
to attend the chapel. The preached word was a
Divine power, and in the second year of my settlement, in 1840, he joined the church, and gave himself to Christian work. All through the forty-six
years—for he is still living—he has been most
consistent, and as far as known there is not a blot
on his character. For many years he was an office-
bearer and Sabbath-school teacher. Although of a
phlegmatic temperament, he has within gracious

tenderness and sterling principle—no time-server, no weather Christian, but true to Jesus under all circumstances. He stood by the church amid every change, and helped to guide it into peaceful waters. He is not satisfied with surface thought, but would dip deep in the Bible mine for golden nuggets, was considered religiously intelligent, hence well fitted to examine candidates for church membership. That he continues to have the Christian asssurance that casts out fear—making him, as he used to say, dread death as little as he did sleep, may be inferred from these words in a letter received—" I am still hoping on. Jesus is very precious. The end is drawing nearer, and hope is brighter and brighter." May his setting sun be full of the light and splendour of Jesus—HIS Cross be the one object of gaze and trust !

One other person may be mentioned. Received into the church a poor lad; by sobriety, industry, shrewdness and thrift, with God's blessing, he has risen in the world, and become an employer. For many years he was a spiritual good—attentive to the means of grace, active in the Sabbath school, and a liberal supporter of the cause. In latter years, we regret to say, there have " been roots of bitterness." Would to God these were plucked up, and that oneness, prayerfulness, and holy consistency abounded !

As far as known, there are now (1886) living only twelve who were members of the first church. From 70 to 80, I trust, died in the faith of the Gospel; their spirits have gone to the " Jerusalem

F

above," and their bodies are in the grave waiting the resurrection morn.

" The saints of God, from death set free,
    With joy shall mount on high ;
The heav'nly hosts with praises loud
    Shall meet them in the sky.

" Together to their Father's house
    With joyful hearts they go ;
And dwell for ever with the Lord,
    Beyond the reach of woe.

" A few short years of evil past,
    We reach the happy shore,
Where death-divided friends at last
    Shall meet, to part no more."

CHAPTER IX.

Second Pastorate.

"A clergyman is a nondescript in heraldry — a singular anomaly, yet one convertible to the noblest duties and the happiest results, and eminently conducive to the healthful state of the body politic. But the true and essential business of a Christian teacher has for its aim a loftier object, a wider range, and looks above and beyond a perishable world. This is his specific character: his lessons are preparative for death; his pulpit, the school of immortality."—DR. CHALMERS.

MY second pastorate, begun in December, 1846, when thirty years old, was in a town in Devonshire, situated on a hill surrounded by lovely scenery. In the day of the great John Howe, who preached in it, it was called "Gospel corner." The congregation, considering the population, was good and influential; never could people be more considerate and kind. Twelve stations in connection with the church were weekly supplied by lay brethren. Their first minister, who was abundant in labour, laid down the rule that all having gifts must "talk for Jesus;" hence the preachers were "plentiful as blackberries," as said an eminent minister. It was my duty and privilege to visit these stations as often as convenient; and, as the distances between them were from four to ten miles a pony and trap were provided. The pony was white—from its colour and use was called "the Gospel pony;" and, as it occasionally fell, through weakness of its knees, people said it was fond of knee-work.

At all the numerous social gatherings and public meetings I was expected to take a principal part.

A quarterly meeting held alternately at the stations was full of interest. Many came together for prayer, business, social tea, and a revival service. They were "red letter days," when holy influences were felt and saving good done. Only the records of the "great day" can reveal the blessed results!

There was the usual routine of Sabbath services in the chapel. An early prayer meeting at seven o'clock; preaching in the forenoon and evening; a public catechetical service in the afternoon from three to four, attended by the school children and others; afterwards, the "holy communion;" and the services of the day were concluded by a short prayer meeting. During the week two meetings were held, one for prayers and the other for exposition. One or two nights were occupied at one or other of the stations.

It is cause for thankfulness that harmony reigned in the church and that there were additions time after time to the membership. No church for its size could have had a better supply of helpers. We were specially blessed by a number of excellent Christian ladies, whose meat and drink it was to do God's will. They were women of prayer, ready with gifts, of moral influence, and abounding in religious effort.

On week evenings lectures were delivered and well received. Some of the subjects were :—" The Wonderful Book;" "Luther on the Reformation;" "Bunyan and Persecution for Conscience' Sake;" "John Knox and Scotland's Struggles;" "Howard and Prisons;" "Wilberforce and practical Christianity;" "Carey and Bible Translation;" "Galileo and the Solar Spots;" "Newton and the Law of Gravitation;" "Herschell and the Telescope;" "Watt and Steam;" "Harvey and the Circulation of the Blood;" "Hunter and the Human Frame," etc. Most of the lectures were illustrated by diagrams. Some thirty years after their delivery the mayor of the town, meeting me, referred to the pleasure and profit he had in attending them. At that time he was a boy in the Sabbath school. Others have spoken with interest of the lectures.

One member of the church, who died 15th March, 1857, I must mention. He preached the Gospel in the town before there was a church of his faith and order ; and, coming to reside permanently in the place, was one of the chief supports of the cause. He not only gave liberally towards the support of the minister, but was incessant in other labours. Every Lord's-day he would be seen riding off to supply one or other of the stations, miles from his own home. His ministrations were not only much valued, but greatly blessed in conversion. Not a few will be his crown of rejoicing in the "day of the Lord." It was my melancholy privilege to bury him, and to preach the funeral sermon, afterwards published by request. Its title was "The Faithful Servant."

The persons attending the chapels in the villages and hamlets had variety in their teaching. The brethren who spoke to them differed in matter and manner. Some had had a good education, others an imperfect one; some were pathetic, and sought with tears to win to Christ; others, boisterous and driving, would impel the sinner to flee from the wrath to come; some excelled in anecdote, others in simple statement; some were fluent, others slow in speech; some were doctrinal, others experimental, and others practical. Whatever the difference, each in his own way sought to lead sinners to the Saviour, and to be a good to saints. Great praise is due to these lay preachers. After the toils of the week, instead of resting at home on Lord's-day, they cheerfully visited the stations, and without fee preached as God enabled them. They had their reward in doing good, and they will have the "faithful and well done," on the day of judgment.

My dear wife was spared for eleven years after my settlement in the town. Though continually feeble, her motto ever was, "At it; always at it." She abounded in the work of the Lord, and as in the first pastorate so now was active in the Sabbath school, in maternal meetings, in religious visitation, and in tract distribution. When unable to meet her Bible-class in school it met in her sick-room. When confined to bed, and nearing Spirit-land, she was full of religious joy. Never was it our privilege to see Grace *so* triumph over weakness and pain, making the sick-room the portal of heaven. There was victory over sin and death and the grave. Lying in the " arms of Jesus," she had glory in the soul. She died a few days after " the faithful servant " mentioned above, and, by her request, was buried by his side. Both sleep in Christ, waiting the sound of the trumpet. " Agnes Gray ; or, Glorifying Christ in Life and Death," a tract published by the Religious Tract Society, contains a short account of her life and dying experiences.

It was while residing in Devonshire that my dear parents " fell asleep "—distance prevented my seeing them in their last days. My father died in 1847, and mother in 1853. Both had passed their three-score-and-ten years. They are now with their Lord and Saviour, within the veil, unspeakably happy.

> " How bright these glorious spirits shine !
>   Whence all their white array ?
> How came they to the blissful seats
>   Of everlasting day ?
> Lo ! these are they from sufferings great,
>   Who came to realms of light,
> And in the blood of Christ have washed
>   Those robes which shine so bright."

In the year 1856 I was appointed by the Devon Association of Baptist Churches to prepare what is called " The Circular Letter " for their next meeting of ministers and delegates, to be held at Torquay in June, 1857, the subject being, " The Sabbath School, and its Aspects to the Church and the World." It was read, adopted, and printed, with other Association matters, for circulation among the churches.

It was also published in a separate form by Messrs. Judd & Glass, London, having the following advertisement;—" The 'matter' in the following pages was prepared for local circulation; but the writer having been urged by brethren to print it in a general form, for wider use, he hopes that their kind opinion of its excellence and adaptation for usefulness will be appreciated by a reading public. May God bless this weak effort for His glory!"

During this pastorate, in 1850, the country was greatly excited by the Bull of the Pope, in which he mapped out England, appointing bishops and archbishops to the different districts. Meetings were everywhere held, addresses given, and petitions to Her Majesty written and signed by hundreds and thousands. Persons would have the strong arm of authority put forth, forbidding the Pope's assumption. I was asked but refused to sign a requisition to our Mayor to call a public meeting. To vindicate my action in this matter this address was printed and widely circulated:—

"Having refused to sign the requisition to the Mayor, in which he is requested to call a meeting of the inhabitants of this town, to address Her Majesty on the supposed Papal aggressions, that I may not be misunderstood, I pen a few thoughts. It would have been a gratification to have acted in concert with other Christian friends; but I cannot violate the law of conscience or the rule of duty. I have no sympathy with that feeling of alarm that runs through the heart of society. To me it appears imaginary. The bull of 'Pius the last,' in which he maps out England, appointing bishops and arch-bishops, has to my mind no terrors. When it is remembered that the Pope had to flee his own domains in disguise, and that his present seat is propped by bayonets—that the Romish hierarchy is shaken to its centre, and that its days are numbered, I have too great confidence in the Christianity of this nation, to join in the wail cry. Religion is not in danger—the throne of our beloved Queen is not seated on the mouth of Ætna, so that Englishmen need not with faggots and effigies, in vestry-meetings, and town-halls, cry, 'Stop the bull—address Her Majesty—ask from her the adoption of legitimate measures for its repression; and, if needs be, let a new law be created, to blot out the Pope's territorial lines, to tear the cap from the head of the cardinal, and to banish the bishops and archbishops of the Romish See.' Are these the days of the middle ages? Must we go back to the dark times, when men were forbidden to *think*—when, forsooth, there must be uniformity; when the subjects of this realm were taxed, and fined, and banished, and burned, if they should have what was called a NON-conforming creed? Alas! for beloved England!

"Fellow-townsmen, pause before you proceed. If you are Protestant Dissenters, take care that you do not sign away your own birthright. We do not ask you to favour Popery;—it is a dark, antichristian system—red with the blood of the saints—superstitious and idolatrous:—it would blot out the light of God's truth, and give night to our world;—it would bind body and soul, and make you a mean serf.

But use not weapons for its overthrow which may one day be wielded against you. That carnal arm in which you may now be disposed to trust—the sword you would take from its scabbard, may be lifted up against your religious rights. 'They that take the sword shall perish with the sword.' As the Romish bull is not an attack upon the Throne, or your civil rights as the subjects of the best of Queens, but rather an assault on the hierarchy—one church at war with another, let the titled bishops and their children fight their own battles.

"We fear not the issue. The God of heaven reigneth. Truth is eternal and omnipotent. Let your weapons against popery be only those that are spiritual. Discuss, preach, pray. 'Luther-like, nail the theses to the hall-door;' and challenge a war of thought. Let the Gospel—justification by faith, be preached through the length and breadth of the land. Live Christianity; and as the child of Him who is the 'Prince of Peace,' sheathe your carnal sword, convert it into an olive branch, and pray ' Father, forgive them; for they know not what they do.' If you desire the salvation of the many millions of your Roman Catholic subjects, create not a mountain barrier by the dip of your pen. Excite not their prejudice, and close the door of their hearts to Divine light. Meet them in the spirit of Christian kindness ; and say, 'I cannot take from you what I claim for myself—a right to private judgment, and free religious action.' If you would not countenance the Pope in his cruel iniquisitions, return good for evil; adopt not his persecuting word, by saying, ' You must not map out our country for ecclesiastical purposes.' This is not Christian, it is papal;—it is not Christ-like, it is Pope-like;—it is not the spiritual weapon of truth, it is the carnal weapon of the state.

" Fellow-townsmen, you may be told that the Pope seeks to rob you of your civil rights. This is only an assumption;—it has no place in the published bull. We know that the spirit of popery is cruel—we cannot forget the fires it has kindled, the gibbets it has erected, and the deep dungeons it has filled with the faithful of the earth; but as it is only the open act that the law recognises, run not to the punishment of a man who may only be a traitor at heart. ' The moment the treason appears in speech or act, then let the police do their duty. Then let the Cardinal's hat be no more a protection than the poorest beaver that ever covered an offender's head.' Ponder well the following words, penned by a great thinker :—' The Romish church and all other churches are, as to this matter, in the same boat. The principle which brings freedom to them is the same which brings freedom to ourselves. The chains which are forged for Romanists to-day, may be forced on Dissenters to-morrow. If Noncon-formists do not hold fast the principle of religious liberty in its fullest extent, they or their children will be likely to rue the day when they abandoned it. If we should unhappily lend ourselves to legisla-tion against the religious liberties of Romanists, we should deserve in the next session of Parliament to lose our own.'

"Fellow-dissenters and townsmen, it is for you now to act in accordance with your convictions of truth and right. I feel that I have done my duty. I may stand alone in this matter, and become a word for the orator; still I have a conscience erect; and shall never stoop to forge one link to bind any of the souls or bodies of Her Majesty's subjects;—shall never give my word to favour any hierarchy to the injury of another;—shall never say to the ministers of any denomination, begone from our shores. Farewell;—wishing you every good."

During the twelve years of pastoral work there was true concord between the ministers of the district. The brethren were joined to each other in affection, sympathy, work, and loving, generous home-receptions. The majority of these are sleeping in their graves; but their memories are dear, and there is fellowship with their glorified spirits Although *up there* with Christ, they are *down here* with us in gracious ministrations. I cannot believe in the separation of spirits. The two or three brethren who still live, although gone from the district, are very dear, and are constantly remembered. The *past* is to me a *present;* so that now there are mental memories of happy hours spent together.

Oh! the glad, glad, years of this second pastorate are sunshine, with one dark shadow—the death of my dear wife.

Among the small books published during this pastorate were, "The Bleeding Heart; or, I am

Anxious," a copyright book, and the fourth volume
of " The Christian's Pocket Library;" " Heaven on
Earth to Me; or, The Cross of Jesus." A third,
" Words of Life; or, Why Not be Saved?" A
fourth, " A Sight of Christ; or, The Sinner's Blessedness." This last was valued by a Christian physician,
who purchased many copies for gifts to his patients.
I also wrote a few articles for *The Evangelist*,
published in Glasgow. These books may have
proved " bread cast upon the waters," to be seen
after many days !

CHAPTER X.

A Travelling Agent.

"How a man acts about money—how he makes it, spends it, saves it, keeps it, thinks about it—is one of the best tests of his moral and spiritual state; so that, as Henry Taylor says, in his thoughtful 'Notes from Life,' a right measure and manner in getting, saving, spending, giving, taking, lending, borrowing, and bequeathing, would almost argue a perfect man."

"IF you wish to doubt Christianity, become a collector for a religious society." Why this saying? Because the *money* test is one of the strongest of religion; and pelf has firm hold of the heart. If the "love of money" has been destroyed—if generousness fills the life—if we give to the poor as lending to the Lord—if we believe that it is more blessed to give than to receive, *then* we make it manifest that we have conquered self and mammon. But if we are churlish and illiberal, men see that we have not Christ's grace, and are belying our religious professions. What are we to think of the professor who receives a collector for benevolent purposes with a scowl, an angry word, and closed pockets? Either that he is a hypocrite, or that religion is not a power. It is *selfish* actions that make infidels.

Did Jesus ever receive the needy with harshness? was there a frown on His face and cold words on His lips? Once with seeming harshness He said to the Canaanite woman, "It is not meet to take the children's bread and to cast it to dogs." But there was a gracious purpose in these words; and behind the seeming frown there was a smiling face. Christ by testing faith, would prove to all ages what *urgency* can do; and make the woman a blessed example to Christians. She occupies the pedestal of immortality, on which is written, "Lord, help me;" with the other words, "O woman, great is thy faith: be it unto thee even as thou wilt."

About thirteen months after the death of my dear wife, I considered it my duty to re-marry. My spouse was the daughter of the "Faithful Servant" mentioned in a former chapter.

At this very time I was asked to become the travelling agent of the Bible Translation Society, an office which I accepted. My duties were to visit districts in England, Wales, and Scotland, collect for its funds, and when occasion offered to preach. This necessitated frequent absence from home, and intercourse with many professed Christians, some of whom received me coldly, others warmly, and others were "neither cold nor hot." I had, however, few refusals. Of the incidents which happened in visitation, I venture to record a few.

My first visit was to a generous gentleman in Scotland. Having heard me preach on Sabbath, and knowing my mission, he expected a call, and received me most cordially. He freely entered into conversation, and was in no haste for my departure.

He was told that we were anxious to raise the income to a figure then mentioned; and that we would be thankful for increased help. As nearly as I can remember he said,—" Well Mr. ———, I have in past years given"—I think it was—" £25, I will now give you £100; and if you get others to increase in the same proportion your wish will be accomplished." My thankful surprise was expressed, but full of humbleness he said—"No thanks are needed. It is a good cause, and I feel a pleasure in giving."

For years he gave me annually £100. Our noble-minded Christian now rests in the grave; but his loving look is still present to the mind. Mr. David Dale used to say, " I gave my money to God in handfuls, and He gave it back to me in shovelfuls." Our Christian friend had a similar experience; he gave away his money in hundreds and thousands, and when he died we were told he was worth three millions.

Another gentleman who lived in Yorkshire, received me with great cordialness. He paid his subscription with willingness; and on my returning thanks, said,—"Oh! you must not thank me; I ought to thank you for the opportunity of giving." What sunshine there would be on the " hard life " of a " religious beggar," if all subscribers acted in a similar way!

A third in the same county said,—" I don't look upon giving as a duty—it is a privilege and I consider it as such. I think Christians ought to take the higher platform, and give to God's cause

from a sense of privilege." If *privilege* was the
platform of all duty, how the "yoke" and the
"burden" of life would be "light" and "easy!"—
the bitter would be a sweet, and the cross a felt joy.
Many other cases might be given. A somewhat
peculiar case happened in a far north city. The
gentleman upon whom I waited was of a generous
yet hasty spirit. He received me with a scowl and
the words :—" I do not intend giving you anything.
Some of the Committee of —— Society, have
injured my feelings, and I feel aggrieved." He was
reminded that the Society named was different from
the one that now asked his help, and that it ought
not to suffer because of the grievance. " Oh !" said
he, " both Societies are managed by the same men."
He continued to speak in angry tones, and I left
him pained and sadly cast down, but ere I had gone
many yards from his works, one of his men came
running after me, saying " Mr. —— wishes to see
you." When I went back, the good man took me
by the hand, and uttered some such words :—" I am
sorry for what I said, and ask your forgiveness.
Here is five pounds for your Society." What a
change ! There was sunshine on the face, kindness
in the spirit, and sweetness in the words. The
storm was over, and there was a peaceful calm.
We left each other with smiles.

In one of our counties there is a large chapel,
situated on high ground, attended by many wealthy
families. The people have the name of being strict
in doctrine and communion. Connected with the
place is a smoking-room ; the interval between the

G

morning and afternoon services is spent in smoking and discussing the sermon. They weigh the discourse in their balances, and, if found wanting, the minister is likely to know of it. As an ordeal or discipline, we were told, students in a certain college were sent there as a supply. They knew that their sermons would have severe criticism; and, failing in matter or manner, they might suffer a rebuke. Thus the place was a dread.

The members of this church were friends of the Society I represented, and offered a collection if I would preach. This I consented to do. At the date fixed I went with fear and trembling. When in the pulpit, looking round on the congregation, I was struck by the many aristocratic persons present, said to be worth their hundreds of thousands. They had keen, intelligent, genial faces. The singing was hearty, and the prayer tended to compose the mind. The text was, " He shall see of the travail of His soul, and shall be satisfied" (Isaiah liii. 11). Divine help was afforded, and I felt so full of the subject that I forgot the critical character of my hearers. There was marked attention, and seemingly they were satisfied. On leaving, one of the deacons—venerable, and a true Puritan—shook hands with me, and said, " Mr. ———, you have left the pulpit-door open, and we will be pleased to see you again. Sometimes ministers come here and preach such sermons that they close the pulpit-door; and we have no wish to see or hear them again. Not so with you." This was strength to my " feeble knees." As showing that the imperfect services were valued

I was frequently asked to preach, when collections were made for the Society.

In my travels I called upon a gentleman who may be considered an extreme type of the niggard. Money seemed his god, at least he parted with it reluctantly. A Christian minister told me that this person had been known to shed tears on losing a shilling. He had been blessed with a generous Christian wife of personal means, a friend of Bible translation, who left to the Society a reversionary legacy of £500, with the condition that her husband yearly pay £5—one per cent. of interest on amount. He would have eluded the payment could he have legally done so. To secure the money he must be waited on; and there was the difficulty of finding him, as he nearly every day attended market, returning late at night, so that to make the call successful he had to be seen at an unreasonable hour in the morning, about seven or eight o'clock. He paid the contribution by cheque, minus income-tax, dating it some days in advance to secure the item of interest on the amount. Let it not be supposed that this gentleman was needy. No; he was a man of property, whose grand idea was to gather money, not to give it away. Alas! he had none of the sweets of Christian giving; the blessing of those ready to perish did not come upon him.

The fifteen years spent as a " religious mendicant " had trials and pleasures. Frequently jaded in mind and body, at other times refreshed by kindness, but for these years I never could have made so many friends, preached in so many places, nor seen so many cities and towns, which greatly increased my knowledge of character and country.

I may mention that during ten years of my second pastorate and fifteen as travelling agent—in all, twenty-five—I was secretary of an Auxiliary for Home and Foreign Missions. On vacating office, I had a handsome presentation of books.

During the first nine years of my travelling days, our home was in a small antique town of about 3,000 inhabitants. It was pleasantly situated, having interesting land and sea views. From thence we removed to a romantic village in a lovely valley in the same county. Here we lived for six years. In both places we formed hallowed, happy friendships, and for services rendered I received a number of valuable presents. We mention these acts of kindness in justice to Christian friends, who were so very generous to one of the weakest of Christ's servants.

CHAPTER XI.

Last Pastorate.

"The CROSS is the strength of a minister. I, for one, would not like to be without it for the world. I should feel like a soldier without arms, like an artist without his pencil, like a pilot without a compass, like a mechanic without his tools. . . . Give me the Cross of Christ. This is the only lever which has ever turned the world upside down hitherto, and made men forsake their sins. And if this will not, nothing will."—BISHOP RYLE.

THE principal changes in my life have come as surprises. It was especially so at this time. How true the words, "I will bring the blind by a way that they knew not: I will lead them in paths that they have not known: I will make darkness light before them, and crooked things straight. These things will I do unto them, and not forsake them" (Isaiah xlii. 16).

Settled with my family in a village said to be "out of the world," a letter was received from my first church, asking me to become its pastor; and in some such words as, "This was your first place, and the members are anxious you should make it your last."

Tired with so much travel and such frequent absence from home—"*first-love*" being also excited—I readily accepted the invitation, and entered on the pastorate July 13, 1873. The text of my first address was, "For we preach not ourselves, but Christ Jesus, the Lord" (2 Cor. iv. 5). In the afternoon we observed the ordinance of the Supper. It was a season of sacred enjoyment. The evening text was, "There standeth One among you whom ye know not: He it is who, coming after me is preferred before me, whose shoe-latchet I am not worthy to unloose" (John i. 26, 27).

In the discharge of ministerial work it has ever been my desire to make Christ the "alpha and omega" of preaching. Hence on the first Sabbath HE was the subject-matter.

The devotion of the priests of Rama to their god is great. A missionary tells us, "Sitting down it is Rama; and rising up, it is Rama; sleeping, it is Rama; and waking, it is Rama." And, surely sitting, rising, sleeping, or waking, it should be with all Christian priests, "Christ Jesus, my Lord and Saviour!"

The Rev. Dr. Clifford in words full of pathos and power says :—"The facts of Christianity are its power, and Christ Himself is the living core of the facts—that is, Christ is Christianity—and He is the power of God and the wisdom of God. To find power, then, we have not to invent God or to discover Him, but to sit at the feet of Jesus. There God is! The idea of God embodied—'God was in Christ.' That is the eternal, world-illuming fact, and God was in Him for the one supreme purpose of reclaiming the world unto Himself by the ineffably God-like process of not imputing unto men their trespasses. God in Christ—in the Babe and the Man, in His teaching and working, His living and dying and rising again—not the incarnation only, nor the beautiful life only, but the vicarious Life and Death, and Resurrection and Ascension, are the vital efforts of a life-giving and powerful ministry. Gethsemane and Calvary are the key to history, the solution of the problem of Providence, the light of the past, the hope of the future, the removal of sin, the solace for sorrow, and the life of the dead. These are the focal points of all revelation, the suns of great systems of force, the spring-heads of unfailing power. *We must therefore preach Him.* Never did men need Christ more—the actual, suffering, holy Christ dying and living again for sinners. Preach the word—its facts, its biographies, its songs; but chiefly preach the eternal Word—the Christ, the Son of God, Brother of the race, universal Teacher, Reconciler and Saviour, once crucified but now ascended on high. A ministry that does not root itself in the instructive, vicarious, and spiritual facts of the Gospel is as surely doomed to failure and death as that of the physicist who dreams dreams, and never handles the minerals and oils of the laboratory, and brilliantly speculates, but never conducts an experiment."

As it was nearly thirty years since I left the church, great changes had taken place. Few of the old members were living, and the children and young people that were in the Sabbath school during the first pastorate had passed their meridian. There

was not that spiritual life in the church I expected
—only one meeting in the week, and that badly
attended. Worldliness had interfered with healthy
godliness. True, there were some prayerful, loving,
active spirits, who were fully alive to duty, and
were a comfort and stay to the minister; but others
were Laodiceans and took little interest in spiritual
duties. Being secular in spirit, they discouraged
earnest, prayerful effort.

The right-minded in the church, who had the
talent and opportunity, helped in the Sabbath
school and in cottage meetings, and encouraged the
delivery of lectures. The God of all grace gave His
blessing. Although not so many additions as during
my first pastorate, when the church was numerically
weaker, still a few dozens were added. Oh! had
there been the prayer and fervour and consistency
of the *first* members, with the increased money
influence and numbers, what an amount of good
might have been done! God would indeed have
blessed us and made us blessings!

In the seventh year of this settlement it was
my melancholy pleasure to bury the oldest
member of the church. He was the first person
to whom I was introduced in 1839, then living
in the chapel cottage. Not at this time a
member, he became one shortly afterwards. He
was an active worker in the Sabbath school, in
cottage and temperance meetings, and was full of
prayer. Through the forty years of his church
membership he was a consistent Christian. People
talked of him as " a good man." He was for years

a deacon. It was his joy to see his wife and their eight children followers of Christ. I felt a pleasure and a profit in visiting him when on his death-bed. Great was his joy when, two or three days before dying, hand in hand, we repeated the words—

" Soldier of Christ, hold fast,
The war will soon be past;
When victory comes at last,
We'll meet in glory."

There was illumination in the face and a glow all through the spirit. We saw him twice on the day but one before his departure, when he spoke to us such words as : " I am depending on Christ, and not afraid to die; I believe it would be gain. This life is now a burden, and I desire to go to Jesus." Although having lived a comparatively blameless life, he felt guilty and worthless in the presence of Infinite Purity, and only hoped for heaven through the Person and Work of Christ. Hence, during his last night, he kept repeating the words—

" Just as I am, without one plea,
But that Thy blood was shed for me,
And that Thou bidst me come to Thee,
O Lamb of God, I come."

At a quarter to five on Sabbath morning he fell asleep in Jesus, his spirit entering on the blessed services of the eternal Sabbath in the skies. His funeral sermon was preached to a large congregation on Lord's-day evening, 17th April, 1881, from the words, " And I heard a voice from heaven saying unto me, Write, Blessed are the dead which die in the Lord from henceforth: Yea, saith the Spirit, that they may rest from their labours; and their works do follow them " (Rev. xiv. 13).

For seven years I laboured with some degree of comfort. There were seeming harmony and satisfaction with the ministry. In the eighth year, I am sorry to say, there was restlessness with a few. The preaching to them had too much of Christ, and was too personal. Never was an individual grievance taken into the pulpit; and my desire was that the sermon should speak home to each heart. This was the bitterest trial of my life, and gave constant heaviness of spirit. Oh, that I could have encouraged myself more in God, and had less dependence on the creature—made Jesus the Arm of my strength and the Sun of my life !

It is told of Sir Matthew Hale that he dismissed a jury because he was convinced that it had been illegally chosen to favour the Protectorate. Cromwell was highly displeased; and when Sir Matthew returned from the circuit, the Protector told him in anger, that he was not fit to be a Judge. The good Judge answered, " It is very true." Well may ministers of Jesus possess the same meek spirit, and say to the disaffected who question their ability, " It is very true." " Who is sufficient for these things ? "

A Bible class numbering from thirty to forty gave encouragement. Its members had, at our house, an annual social gathering, which was much enjoyed. It was a kind of free-and-easy—having music and recreations.

During the last year of settlement I suffered from deafness, which led me to resolve not to seek another church. It was my wish, however, to preach as occasion offered, and give attention to reading and writing.

On Sabbath, 26th March, 1882, I preached my last sermons :—the text in the morning being, " Now the God of peace, that brought again from the dead our Lord Jesus, that Great Shepherd of the sheep through the blood of the everlasting covenant, make you perfect in every good work to do His will, working in you that which is well-pleasing in His sight, through Jesus Christ, to whom be glory for ever and ever. Amen " (Heb. xiii. 20, 21). The words of discourse at night were, " Fear not ; I am the first and the last " (Rev. i. 17). This last day of sacred service had its shadows ; but I thank God for the grace and strength given.

Amongst the many estimable persons whose friendship made dear the last pastorate, I remember with loving gratitude the following :—

A gentleman and his lady who were great helps in Christian work. Both had interesting Bible classes—one for young men and the other for young women. The gentleman had rare business parts, was a large employer, and a magistrate : but although full of secular work, he was ever in his place in God's house and the school.—a pattern of regularity and punctualness. His excellent lady, besides her church and school duties, was active in temperance work. She was the president of one of the branches of the British Women's Temperance Society. They had a son, a member of the church, full of benevolent action, and of great influence over the young.

A Christian brother, who was to me as my right
arm, a true minister's friend, seemed an essential
in the church and school. He, too, had an excellent
wife who was a true "mother in Israel." We can
say of them—"Greet Priscilla and Aquila, my
helpers in Christ Jesus." Thank God, their one son
bids fair, through grace, to be of great service in the
church.

Another member was full of religious energy, active
in the church and school, and could be depended
on for prayer and help. He removed from the township, but continued his membership. May he and
his family have fulness of blessing!

The mother of a Sabbath school scholar—noted for
strange, odd ways—it was my privilege, during the
first pastorate, to receive into the church. She had
to fight strong opposition from her husband; but
being a woman of remarkable religious nerve, she
conquered. This son, who spoke of her in glowing
words of love and gratitude, joined the church in
1848, and has for many years evinced great interest
in its welfare. May God give him every needed
good!

At the same time a young man was added to the
church. He, too, was a scholar in the Sabbath
school, apt in answering questions, inquisitive, and
fond of study. "Excelsior" was his motto. Without a schoolmaster he conquered difficulties, and
became versed on many subjects; we believe he is
able to read several languages. He became a
minister, has had three pastorates, but is now
retired because of ill-health. We are glad to see

from the newspapers that he continues to " battle
for the truth," using a sharp sword. May he
ever be " strong in the Lord and in the power of
His might ! "

In the last years of the pastorate I was one of the
Nonconformist ministers who conducted a service
in the Union. There was another service by clergymen of the Church of England on a different day.
Thus there was no need for a paid chaplain. We
trust these services were a spiritual good to the
inmates ; and that God was honoured by them.

The township had greatly changed from the time
of my first settlement. The population had doubled ;
and whereas in 1839, there were only three places
of worship there were now ten, and two mission
halls. My friends, too, have built a large school-room
and minister's house. Surely, with such increased
opportunities for good, there ought to be much
religious light and life in the place. *Is it so ?*

While pastor in this district I was asked to write
a short memoir of a Christian brother with whom I
was associated in religious work in Devon. The life
was written—its title being :—" The Border Land
of Heaven : or, the Blessedness of Religion. A true
sketch."

Being asked to pay my old friends a visit on 7th
January, 1883, I did so. Fourteen persons having
to be baptized, it was their wish I should administer
the ordinance. On the evening of the sacred day
were gathered together the largest congregation
ever before known at the place ; the gates had to be

closed against scores who desired entrance. It was a solemn season.

In the afternoon we had the Communion service, with " Christ within the doors."

The discourse of the morning may be considered my prayer for the church: " And let the beauty of the Lord our God be upon us: and establish Thou the work of our hands upon us; yea, the work of our hands establish Thou it" (Psalm xc. 17).

Whatever may have been the shadows of the last pastorate, the people and township can never be forgotten. They have a large place in my thoughts and best wishes. Past days, past scenes, past fellow-ships, past co-operation, are present to the mind; and, were my highest aspirations realized, the church and congregation would be distinguished by holiness and usefulness.

> " Now for my friends and brethren's sakes,
>   Peace be to thee, I'll say,
> And for the house of God our Lord,
>   I'll seek thy good alway."

CHAPTER XII.

Associations and Fellowships.

"When in this vale of years I backward look,
And miss such numbers—numbers, too, of such
Firmer in health and greener in their age,
And stricter on their guard, and fitter far
To play life's subtle game—I scarce believe
I still survive.   And am I fond of life
Who scarce can think it possible I live?"

YOUNG.

"LET Glasgow flourish by the preaching of the Gospel." True to its motto, the City on the Clyde has flourished; and we believe it owes its prosperity to the "righteousness that exalteth a nation." Few cities have grown so rapidly in numbers and wealth and benevolence. In 1740 the population was only 17,034; when I first knew it, it numbered over 200,000; now, with its suburbs, it is 704,436. Its trade, commerce, and shipping have increased indefinitely; its industries are so varied and numerous that there are openings for the diligent of every age and class; its colleges and schools give it a first place in letters; its Gospel ministers rank high for piety, learning, and usefulness; and its philanthropies meet every phase of human ill. For its waifs and outcasts, and unfortunates and inebriates, and its every moral and physical evils, there was a " door of hope "—institutions that met every case. The noonday prayer-meeting is the ladder that joins the city to the Throne of God, and forms clouds full of blessing, making fruitful the commercial city.

During the years I lived in Glasgow there was a race of fine Gospel preachers, whose names and forms fill the mind. There was the quaint, outspoken, interesting Dr. William Anderson; the sonorous, vivid Dr. Beattie; the fervid, eloquent Dr. Chalmers; the fascinating, angelic Greville Ewing; the neat, upright Dr. Heugh; the scholarly, concise Dr. King; the nimble-footed, brisk Dr. Kidston; the model, prim Dr. Mitchell; the weighty, grave Dr. Struthers; the chaste, silvery Dr. Wardlaw, with many others too numerous to mention. These great and good men had " understanding of the times," and were spiritual forces. We remember their flow of eloquence by which whole audiences were moved. In the pulpit, when speaking on the wonders of Divine grace; or on the platform, when pleading the cause of philanthropy—the whole man permeated with the theme—what swelling waves of emotion, laughter and smiles, and tears and loud applause. Ah! these were days not to be forgotten.

The visits of the Rev. John Williams from the South Seas, the Rev. Robert Moffat from Africa, and the Rev. William Knibb from Jamaica, were memorable occasions.

Who can forget the crowded, enthusiastic meetings when the South Sea missionary gave his account of " Chips can talk;" or, " Oh, these foreigners, they are roasting stones! they are roasting stones! come hurricane and blow down our bananas and our bread-fruit, we shall never suffer from famine again, these foreigners are teaching us to roast stones!" or, "Poor puss!" "here's a monster from the deep;" or the "Spiritual beggar," who had neither hands nor feet; and other interesting cases that made the heart glow with ecstasy?

What memory has lost the impressions produced by the noble African missionary when he gave the account of his encounters with savages and wild beasts; of the native who must spear the letter, lest it talked to him on the way; of his teaching the alphabet to the tune of "Auld lang-syne;" of the conversion of Africaner; with the incredulity of the farmer who, when told that Africaner was a good man, said, "I can believe almost anything you say, but *that* I cannot credit; there are seven wonders in the world, that would be the eighth," etc., etc.? To see him, with his fine presence and his lion, noble countenance, on the platform, with extended arms, is a picture to carry into eternity, when we hope to gaze on the actual glorified person, made more glorious by the power of the adored Jesus!

Are not the clarion sounds of Mr. Knibb's voice, with its musical swell, when pleading for the emancipation of the West Indian slaves, still ringing in the ears? The *mettle* of the man may be learned from two incidents. On arriving in the English Channel the pilot steps on board, and Knibb's first question is, "Well, pilot, what news?" "The

Reform Bill has passed." "Thank God!" he rejoined. "Now I'll have slavery down. I will never rest, day or night, till I see it destroyed root and branch." At a meeting, his coat being pulled by the secretary of the Baptist Mission as a caution to moderate his words, he said, " Whatever may be the consequences, I *will* speak. At the risk of my connection with the Society, and of all I hold dear, I will avow this: and if the friends of Missions will not hear me, I will turn and tell it to my God; nor will I desist till this greatest of curses is removed and 'Glory to God in the highest' is inscribed on the British flag." It was my privilege to hear this great man in West George Street Church. At one part of his speech, greatly excited, he lifted a chain —the shackle of a poor slave—and with force threw it down on the platform, its clanking sound being heard over the church, and said something like this: "So let the shackle fall and break, and never more pain the wrist or leg of a poor slave. May God give universal freedom!" Imagine, if you can, the effect on the audience; how hearts throbbed, tears filled eyes, and voices gave loud cheers! Hear him also saying, "I have been represented in Glasgow as a grave-digger; but I have come to dig the grave of colonial slavery, to entomb the greatest curse that ever rested on Britain; and I will not leave off till the proud flag of freedom wave victorious over the isles of the West, and till I hear them resound with the impressive cry, 'Africa is free! Hallelujah! Hallelujah! Hallelujah! The Lord God omnipotent reigneth!'"

We believe in Divine inspiration * all through the ages: that God's servants on certain occasions, to work important purposes, had "tongues of fire." How otherwise can we account for such speeches as those delivered by Williams, Moffat, Knibb, and others? They had within them an heavenly impulse that glowed and was unconquerable; the coals and the fire and the refining were from God: and to Him be the glory!

In an important discussion about this time on gradual and immediate emancipation, the disputants were the Rev. Mr. Breckenridge, of America, and George Thompson, Esq. The American divine was a keen, intelligent casuist, an able reasoner of great power, and made the best of a bad cause. For Mr. Breckenridge, who was suffering from an acute pain in the teeth or face—which required the frequent use of a narcotic—much sympathy was felt, but he displayed calm mastery of himself and subject. Undoubtedly he was a great man; but, justice and mercy and fervid eloquence being on the side of Mr. Thompson, he carried the majority of the audience and secured their loudest applause. Men of mark and of different shades of opinion were on the platform.

I was present at an able discussion on Roman Catholicism in West Nile Street Church, but the

---

* The Rev. Dr. Parker might well ask, "If God lives, why should inspiration cease? There may be differences of method in defining inspiration, but as to its substantial meaning and happy uses, inspiration must be continuous with the existence of God— must be the parallel line to the Divine duration."

names of the "men of war" have gone from the memory; not so the name of the chairman, William M'Gavin, Esq., author of "The Protestant," well able to preside, from his big brain and prodigious memory, and to define the swords of the two disputants. Mr. M'Gavin published from memory a nearly verbatim account of the discussion. He had an amanuensis in good Mr. Allan, famed for his quick writing and remarkable ability in figures, said to be able to sum up three money columns at one time. "The Protestant" found in him the " pen of a ready writer," a helper indeed; and was only able by his aid to attend to the many duties that devolved upon him as a banker, author, citizen, and patriot.

At other meetings of an exciting nature the Voluntary Church question, temperance, etc., etc., were discussed. Glasgow was then famed for platform oratory on all questions of interest.

Among the friends of those days memory lingers fondly on the following :—

Mr. HENRY CLOW was among our first associates, and, being fellow-members of the Young Men's Christian Association, meeting in same branch, we had frequent intercourse. He was five years my senior. In my teens I must have been fond of religious speculation, for I well remember that friend Clow, dubious about my orthodoxy, sought to set me right on certain passages of Scripture, in the book of Revelation I think. Difference, if any, in religious opinions did not cool Christian affection, for we continued fast friends. During the cholera epidemic in Glasgow his brother was smitten with the dread disease. Henry, anxious about his soul, asked me to visit him, which, having no fear of contagion, I freely did, prayed, and had religious conversation with him. He recovered, and some time afterwards avowed himself a Christian. Our friendship became more sacred and true. At another time Mr. Clow, when going from home, asked me to take his Sabbath-school class, which I did. Knowing that my friend was a good singer, and that he opened his school with praise and prayer, I thought I must do the same. My first attempt at public singing proved my last, being full of discord, without harmony. The children must have been amazed at the strange sounds, so different from those of their kind teacher's; but there were no manifestations of their feelings, they only sought to help me in my music weakness.

Mr Clow long after this did good Christian service in the city, and was a spiritual force for many years, specially among the young. In the *Young Men's Christian Magazine* for March, 1844, there is an account of "Memorial Service," from which the following is extracted :—

" Mr. Clow was connected with such a number of societies, and carried on such a variety of Christian work, that it will be good to give expression to the manifold experiences of his fellow-workers, which will form a kind of symposium on Mr. Clow's character and work. This was well brought out at the memorial service held in the Christian Institute on Sabbath, 3rd February. There was a large attendance. Mr. George Macfarlane occupied the chair, and, after engaging in devotional exercises, referred to the genial, open, and winning ways of Mr. Clow, and to his long service and connection with the Association. Several friends, who could not be present, sent papers. These have been condensed in the following notes :—

"Rev. Mr. Goodrich: 'He served his own generation. From his youth Henry Clow was devoted to good work. He was connected with the Y.M.C.A. for 56 years, and for 25 years was its president. For 50 years, save one, he was an highly esteemed member of Elgin Place Church; for 21 years he faithfully served it in the office of deacon. He was a good man, full of purpose to do good, and of a cheerful, kindly manner. His special gift of service was this most useful one: the influencing of young men unto good. One useful in the Church has written to me concerning Mr. Clow: 'It was to his faithful, pointed words, spoken to me just at the right time (the very tones, and loving pressure of the hand that accompanied them, come freshly back to me as I write), that I attribute my conscious decision for Christ.' . . . And so our brother beloved served his own generation; not contemning or condemning it, but serving it, and serving it according to God's will; cheerfully acknowledging the goodness of God's law that he should serve; content with the form of service appointed him, and striving to fulfil it faithfully as God's will. He thus won the respect of all and the affection of not a few.'"

"Mr. Oatts said he was privileged to see Mr. Clow two days before he died. Grasping both my hands in his, he testified to the faithfulness of God's word, and wondered how those do who came to die without it. Then with his remaining breath he repeated the text, 'I know whom I have believed, and am persuaded that He is able to keep that which I have committed unto Him against that day.'"

Mr. JOHN SANDS was to me of great religious service. My superior in position, experience, and years, I looked to him for Christian advice, which he was ever ready to give. Sometimes we walked together, and never can I forget the influence these walks had upon my mind. Mr. Sands was full of holy converse. Enoch-like, he ever walked with God. His countenance was an illumination, and out of his heart welled forth gracious words. When with him, you seemed altogether separated from the world, having around you heavenly influences. It made me feel—shall I confess it?—strange; I felt humbled, and earnestly desired to have the same Divine glow of heart and life. Alas! when I think on my friend, I am sometimes disposed to question my Christianity; but there is the precious blood of Jesus—that's my hope!

Mr. Sands, some few years after, left for London, and became a man of large commercial business. In his prosperity he never lost his devotion, but continued humble, holy, and useful. He died suddenly while resting on the sofa, and is now amongst the many who sleep in Jesus.

ROBERT KETTLE, Esq., was to me a spiritual guide. A father in years, he was ever ready to speak kind words and give wise counsel. Of a cheery, frank nature, there was no need for reserve in his presence; indeed his winning look dispelled it. He was well known in Glasgow as one of its first philanthropists—secretary of the City Mission, active in the temperance cause, the first adjudicator of the prize essays on the Sabbath, ready to do all kinds of Christian work, everywhere venerated and beloved. A ready speaker, he was on the platform attractive and racy. Dining and taking tea with him were golden opportunities. He willingly read, corrected, and freely gave his opinion on, any manuscripts submitted to him. We bless God for his association and fellowship. Mr. Kettle's death, 23rd March, 1852, was universally bewailed. "The tidings of his decease spread a gloom over the community. His funeral was attended by large numbers—civic authorities, ministers of varied sects, men foremost in all great movements, were there." In the Necropolis, where he was buried, a public monument was erected to his memory.

An interesting book has been published: "Temperance Memorials of the late Robert Kettle, Esq.; consisting of Selections from his Writings on the Temperance Question. With a Memoir of his Life, by the Rev. William Reid." From that book the following selection is given :—

"His character presented a form of rare symmetry. Happening to mention the name of Mr. Kettle the other day to a Glasgow gentleman, he exclaimed,

'He was a wonderful man!' Now, what made him wonderful? Equal sagacity, equal integrity, equal benevolence, equal humour, might be met with in hundreds whose names have never been known beyond their own little circle. What then was it that constituted Mr. Kettle's superiority? It was the combination, the harmony of the whole. We may have seen qualities of equal strength in others, but seldom have we seen so much of harmony and just proportion in any. None could say of him, He may be very decent, but not very upright; very kind in his givings, but not very charitable in his feelings. That Robert Kettle had his faults we doubt not; but, whatever they were, we never saw them, nor do we expect to see, on this side of death, a nearer approximation to the standard of the Gospel. He was beautiful and strong, because he drew daily at the fountain whence all life and nourishment must be drawn. Travellers tell us of a tree that grows full and vigorous on the deserts of Africa. Strangely does it stand in contrast with the barren, scorching wastes around. In spring it puts forth its tender leaves, and in autumn the thirsty pilgrim is not only pleased with its beauty, but refreshed with its delicious fruit. The mystery is solved when the guide explains that it is of a kind that sends down its roots, in the form of delicate fibres, to a great depth, and then onwards to the river's banks; and thus supplied with never-failing nourishment, it defies the heat of the sultry sun and the tornado of the desert. It was thus that the character of our friend appeared so lovely amid the scenes of

life in which he was appointed to move.   United to
Christ, as the branch is united to the vine, he was
enabled to 'bear much fruit.'"

With another gentleman, a fellow-member of the
Young Men's Society, I had frequent intercourse.
He has risen to giddy heights of success.   When
he began business, it was in a small shop with cellar
beneath.   If I mistake not, I was one of his first
customers.   This good brother was full of *push*;
and his tact, energy, and lawful ambition were to
be rewarded.   The small shop was exchanged for
one considerably larger: the larger soon had wider
extension; and the extended premises on the ground-
floor had to be supplemented with expansive rooms
above.   These afterwards were exchanged for very
large premises in one of the chief streets of the city.
Now my friend has one of the largest and most
successful businesses, lives in a West-end palace, and
has his sea-side residence and pleasant steam yacht.
His excellent lady was full of Christian work
in her maidenhood.   She had her tract district and
a meeting for adults, which I had the pleasure of
addressing.   I trust that in their greatly improved
position they are full of goodness!   "To whom
much is given, of them much shall be required."

A dear friend—the late Mr. JOHN LAMONT—with
whom I had many loving associations and fellowships, and myself, paid a visit to our native town,
Galston, and called on a person who was past his
meridian.   He was a good man, and was so con-

sidered by his neighbours. We received from him a kind welcome and were struck by his pleasant face and the sweet mellowness of his voice. There was soon oneness with the children of the Heavenly King, and our conversation was in accord.

The question that principally engaged our attention was the ministration of the Spirit and of angels : wherein consisted their difference? As my friend and self were striplings, and had little of the knowledge and experience of our elder friend, we left him to answer the question. It would seem that it had engaged much of his thoughts, for he spoke with considerable freedom and decidedness.

He said that the Spirit had to do with *character*; He regenerated, gave gracious strength and support in duty and in trial, and formed the life after the model of Jesus. That the angels had to do with *person*; protecting the body from accident and danger, and, in seasons of mental perplexity, suggesting thoughts that gave immediate relief. He asked if we had never been in great perplexity, not knowing where to look or what to do for deliverance, when a sudden idea would dart into the mind and give instantaneous relief? We both answered that we had been in such a state, greatly perplexed, when by a sudden thought we were relieved.

"That," said he, " was the ministration of angels." He next told us of a godly minister who was much perplexed on the subject of angel-ministration, and made it the subject of earnest prayer. When thus troubled—having laid the question before God—he was asked to visit a sick person. In going to the house he had to ascend an outside stone stair, unprotected by rail.   Praying and conversing with the sick one, he left in haste, deep in thought, and walked over the top-landing of the stair, and fell many feet.   But he might have had an arm around him holding him up, so gentle was the fall, that he received no injury.   This good minister considered this deliverance as the kind ministration of an angel—an answer to his prayer in his own experience.

This recalls a circumstance in my own history. On returning in a trap from a meeting held some eight miles from home, the horse, which was driven by a young friend, became restive, and set off in full gallop, kicking with its hind legs.   Seeing that there must be an upset, I allowed myself to drop from the conveyance, and pitched on my head.   The persons walking behind, who saw the awkwardness of the fall, ran to my assistance, thinking I was seriously injured.   But it was not so.   I might have fallen on a bed of down, I did not feel the least pain in the head or any part of the body.   One of the hind feet of the horse got fixed in a hole it had made in the splash-board, and the animal fell, turning over the vehicle on its side.   Thank God my young driver also escaped unhurt.   The trap and harness were much injured, and we were obliged to walk home.

Bishop Hall thus speaks of the ministration of angels :—" The houses of holy men are full of these heavenly spirits when they know not ; they pitch their tents in ours, and visit us, when we see not ;

and, when we feel not, protect us. It is the honour of God's saints to be attended by angels." Spenser, too, has penned expressive lines on the same subject :—

" How oft do they their silver bowers leave
    To come to succour us that succour want !
How oft do they with golden pinions cleave
    The flitting skies, like flying pursuivants,
Against foul fiends to aid us militant !
    They for us fight, they watch and duly ward,
And their bright squadrons round about us plant,
    And all for love, and nothing for reward.
    Oh ! why should heavenly God to men have such regard ? "

These are questions of some interest: Are the spirits of the departed in Christ engaged in the work of ministration? Do they visit this earth on missions of goodness? We cannot imagine that they are inactive, or that their work is only that of praise. They are said to " follow the Lamb whithersoever He goeth;" and we know that the promise of Christ to His followers on earth is, " Lo, I am with you alway." If this be so—if Jesus is with His people for their good, and departed spirits are following Christ, may not these sainted ones have a share in this mission of goodness? But some may object: " This implies a knowledge of condition on earth, which is full of trouble and sin; would not such a knowledge mar happiness ?" We think not. God's perfect knowledge of all the troubles and evils of the world does not detract from His blessedness; and departed saints may have such likeness to God that, even with this knowledge, they may have perfect enjoyment. We read of coming " to the spirits of just men made perfect;" may not this imply *inter*-association and fellowship? One thing is certain: In Rev. xxii. 8-10, when an angel appeared to John in the isle of Patmos, and made known to him encouraging truth, the awed apostle "fell down to worship before the feet of the angel which shewed him these things," but was forbidden. "Then saith he unto me, See thou do it not: for I am thy fellow-servant, and of thy brethren the prophets, and of them which keep the sayings of this book: worship God." Thus the glorified being was "John's fellow-servant," one of his "brethren" who kept the Divine sayings. Here we find him ministering to the apostle when on earth. Should not this fact teach that in some way the departed minister to us? We speak not dogmatically, but ask the question.

With other Christian friends, too numerous to mention, we have had sweet intercourse and fellowship. The greater number have gone to the happy land. Our spirit has fellowship with their spirits. It may be that they are nearer and more helpful than they were when on earth. We hail the association of the few who are alive, and are pleased with their occasional fellowship. God abundantly bless them, and make them blessings! If their names are not in the Autobiography, memory remembers them with fondness. The *first* fellowships have the glow of youth, and have a place in type, but the printed leaf perishes; whereas memory is undying, and is fadeless and everlasting.

As has been stated, I have been twice married—the union in both instances being blessed with children. My first wife was a true helpmeet for about twenty years. She died in 1857. By her there were four children; only two—a son and daughter—lived to pass the years of maturity. The son now "sleeps in Jesus;" the daughter lives, but is in delicate health. She inherits the Christian devotion of her sainted mother. Married to my present wife over twenty-eight years, in every way she has been, and is, a help and comfort. Of her six children, one dear boy died when seven years old. His last words, when I repeated to him the lines,

> " Gentle Jesus, meek and mild,
>   Look upon a little child ;
>   Pity my simplicity—

were

> *Suffer me to come to Thee."*

The prayer was heard; Jesus did suffer him. "Of such is the kingdom of heaven." The other five are alive—two sons and three daughters. We thank God for them, and pray that each may be kept faithful to Christ to the last hour of human existence; and may we *all* meet around the throne of glory !

> " There have been sweet singing voices
>   In your walks, that now are still ;
>   There are seats left void in your earthly home
>   Which none again can fill.

" Soft eyes are seen no more,
    That made springtime in your heart ;
Kindred and friends are gone before,
    And *ye* still fear to part?

" We fear not now, we fear not !
    Though the way through darkness bends ;
Our souls are strong to follow *them*,
    Our own familiar friends."

CHAPTER XIII.

The Evening of Life.

" Strange that I never felt before
  That I had almost reached my goal.
My bark is nearing death's dark shore,
  Life's waters far behind me roll ;
And yet I love their murmuring swell,
  Their distant breakers' proud array :
And *must* I, *can* I say, ' Farewell ?'
  ' I'm old to-day ! I'm old to-day ! ' "

"THE night is far spent, the day is at hand." It is even so with him who was a " Scotch lad." What remains can only be a few brief years, it may be only a few months. At evening-tide may it be light ! The Day of Glory that knows no end is at hand. On tip-toe let us look out for the first golden rays of the Sun of Heaven !

"Oftentime we look forward with forebodings to *the time of old age*," says Mr. Spurgeon, "forgetful that at eventide it shall be light. To many saints old age is the choicest season in their lives. A balmier air fans the mariner's cheek as he nears the shore of immortality, fewer waves ruffle his sea ; quiet reigns—deep, still, and solemn. From the altar of age the flashes of the fire of youth are gone, but the more real flame of earnest feeling remains.

I

The pilgrims have reached the land of Beulah, that happy country whose days are as the days of heaven upon earth. Angels visit it, celestial gales blow over it, flowers of Paradise grow in it, and the air is filled with seraphic music. Some dwell here for years and others come to it but a few hours before their departure, but it is an Eden on earth. We may well long for the time when we shall recline in its shady groves, and be satisfied with hope until the time of fruition comes. The setting sun seems larger than when aloft in the sky, and a splendour of glory traces all the clouds which surround his going down. Pain breaks not the calm of the sweet twilight of age, for strength made perfect in weakness bears up with patience under it all. Ripe fruits of choice experience are gathered as the rare repast of life's evening, and the soul prepares itself for rest." We read these words with a slight heartache, yet with longing desire to have their full sweet experience.

Unnumbered have been the blessings of a long life —through all the long years mercies which ought to raise songs of thanksgiving. Many imperfections and sins have produced penitence, and caused the soul to cling afresh to Jesus for forgiveness and cleansing. On the border-land of the Invisible, my last confession would be: "Jesus died for sinners; His worthiness is my only plea; with my last gaze I look for His mercy unto eternal life."

The late Dr. Carey, notwithstanding his many mental, moral, and philanthropic excellencies, on his death-bed was asked for the text of his funeral sermon. His humbleness was such that he desired nothing should be said; he would sink into forgetfulness that Christ might be all in all; but he added that, if such a sermon must be preached, the first verse in Psalm li. should be taken: "Have mercy upon me, O God, according to Thy loving-kindness: according to the multitude of Thy tender mercies blot out my transgressions." In harmony with such words, he wished the memorial on his tombstone should be:—

WILLIAM CAREY,

Born, August, 1761. Died, ...

"*A wretched, poor, and helpless worm,*
On Thy kind arm I fall."

Ah! the greatest and the best, as well as the weakest and most worthless, in God's family, are all "chief of sinners."

At the age of sixty-six I relinquished the pastorate and removed to an antique town in Devonshire. Here the evening of life is being spent. It is my privilege occasionally to preach and serve in other Christian work.

This evening of life has what may be called harvest moonlights; for there have been, and are, seasons of reaping and rejoicing. Amongst the number of relatives who have given me light and joy was an elder brother, now no more. He paid us a visit full of gladness. Anxious about a son in failing health in Australia, notwithstanding his great age, he resolved to take the long voyage to see him and another son who was there settled with a wife and family. It was the father's hope to bring the unmarried son back to his native land. Alas! such are the mysteries of Providence! the son died while the father was there; but he had the solace of his father's kind attention in his last hours. Shortly after the father gradually weakened and died too. Both lie in one grave. My brother was seventy-six years old; and, by God's grace, was ripe for heaven. A dear sister and myself, as far as known, are the only two of a large family remaining. My sister is now a widow, having recently been bereaved of her husband. She is the mother of eight living children. We commend her and them to God, who is "the Husband of the widow and the Father of the fatherless." I have other dear orphan nieces and nephews whom I commend to the care of the same gracious Almighty Father.

Among the many friends who give comfort on the down-road of life is a happy family whom I frequently visit. Their home is a Beulah spot, and its surroundings have landscapes and sea views that bring gladness to the heart. It is well to have the evening of life so lit up; but may we never forget that the light they shed is derived; and that by them we "see light in God's light."

Having leisure, I have given some attention to writing articles, tracts, etc. Several of them have been published, and have had, and are having, a wide circulation. During this period a revised edition of "A Sight of Christ" was printed, and soon sold. Besides acting as secretary of the North Devon Auxiliary, being asked, I compiled a History of the Baptist Churches in the district. Two thousand copies were printed, the book favourably noticed, and well received. It was at this time that the idea occurred of filling up my spare moments with writing this Autobiography, knowing that it would be a profitable mental and moral exercise, exciting in me both penitence and praise. It is now given to the world in the hope that, if lives of great men remind us that existence can be made sublime, from these memories of an humble "Scotch lad" a fellow-sinner may derive hope, faith, or encouragement in the battle of life.

God's care is *minute*. He orders our steps. The very hairs of the head are numbered. All our history is written in His book. It may be Providence set me aside from the pastorate for a purpose. Had I continued in it, there would have been little leisure for writing tracts, etc. I claim not for these greatness or even culture; but I trust they have in them the grace and truth of Jesus, and the elements of usefulness. So, by God's blessing, more good may have been done in my last than in my first years. This at least is certain: a greater number has been reached by letterpress than I could have addressed as a pastor. Tens of thousands have had the opportunity of reading what was written. Believing that these writings have Gospel seeds that are incorruptible and will endure for ever, I wait the reaping time, with the words,

" Not unto us, O Lord, not unto us,
  But unto Thy name give glory,
  For Thy mercy and for Thy truth's sake ! "

Gentle reader, farewell! Standing by and hearing the ripple of "the narrow stream of death," and seeing on the other side the pearly gate and the shining ones, I am trustfully looking to Jesus for a glad welcome and a joyful admission into glory. Amen!

> " Life ! I know not what thou art,
>   But know that thou and I must part ;
> And when, or how, or where we met,
>   I own to me 's a secret yet.
> Life ! we've been long together,
>   Through pleasant and through stormy weather ;
> 'Tis hard to part when friends are dear,
>   Perhaps 'twill cost a sigh or tear ;
> Then steal away, give little warning,
>   Choose thine own time :
> Say not Good-night, but in some brighter clime
>   Bid me Good-morning."

"All the Way by which the Lord thy God Led Thee."

> " When we reach a quiet dwelling
>   On the strong eternal hills,
> And our praise to Him is swelling
>   Who the vast creation fills ;
> When the paths of prayer and duty,
>   And affliction, all are trod,
> And we wake and see the beauty
>   Of our Saviour and our God ;

> " With the light of resurrection,
>   When our changed bodies glow,
> And we gain the full perfection
>   Of the bliss begun below ;
> When the life that 'flesh' obscureth,
>   In each radiant form shall shine,
> And the joy that aye endureth
>   Flashes forth in beams Divine ;

" While we wave the palms of glory
 Through the long eternal years,
Shall we e'er forget the story
 Of our mortal griefs and fears?
Shall we e'er forget the sadness,
 And the clouds that hung so dim,
When our hearts are filled with gladness,
 And our tears are dried by Him?

" Shall the memory be banished
 Of His kindness and His care,
When the wants and woes are vanished
 Which He loved to soothe and share?
All the way by which He led us,
 All the grievings which He bore,
All the patient love He taught us,
 Shall we think of them no more?

" Yes! we surely shall remember
 How He quickened us from death,—
How He fanned the dying ember
 With His Spirit's glowing breath.
We shall read the tender meaning
 Of the sorrows and alarms,
As we trod the desert leaning
 On His everlasting Arms.

" And His rest will be the dearer
 When we think of weary ways,
And His light will seem the clearer
 As we muse on cloudy days.
Oh, 'twill be a glorious morrow
 To a dark and stormy day!
We shall recollect our sorrow
 As the streams that pass away."

ANON.